"Here is startling insight on the per within Western culture at large and W Adam Mabry is a pastor and a risi .... who has demonstrated the ability to help people find common ground while maintaining faithfulness to the high calling of obedience to Christ. Refreshingly original, this book deserves serious consideration."

RICE BROOCKS, Co-founder, Every Nation Churches; Bestselling Author, *God's Not Dead* and *The Human Right*

"Our culture's continued descent into polarization and sectarianism presents unique challenges for the church—including our complacency about and contribution to this descent! I'm grateful to my fellow Boston pastor Adam Mabry for his biblical reflection and cultural witness as Christians seek to bear witness to the truth of the gospel and to love our neighbors as ourselves."

STEPHEN T. UM, Senior Pastor, Citylife Presbyterian Church of Boston, MA; The Gospel Coalition Council Member

"I suspect this provocative book will be received with delight and suspicion in equal measure. But for those who long for Christian relationships that go beyond the combative or tribal, and that are instead marked by grace and truth, there's a lot here to make you ponder and pray, with hope and joy."

MARCUS HONEYSETT, Director, Living Leadership

"In an age of social and political ranting, raving, and shouting, Adam Mabry helps God's people learn to reflect, repent, and serve. This is the kind of book that every Christian can read—and, while doing so, every Christian will be both offended and helped."

MARK DRISCOLL, Founding Senior Pastor, The Trinity Church, Scottsdale, AZ; Author, *Win Your War*

"In an age of extremes, Adam Mabry echoes F. Scott Fitzgerald in telling us that the righteous person ought to be able to hold two apparently opposing ideas in their mind at the same time. He is right, and, thank God, he makes his case masterfully in this essential book."

STEPHEN MANSFIELD, New York Times Bestselling Author of *The Faith of George W. Bush* and *Men on Fire*

"Adam Mabry addresses with charity and clarity one of the biggest problems facing the church: the steadfast refusal of most Christians to hold multiple truths in tension with grace. I love how this book models how to think by addressing complicated and pressing questions of theology, discipleship, and cultural engagement with thoughtfulness, openness, and a dedication to biblical truth. You will be challenged as you read, and come away encouraged and chastened. You'll encounter issues that make you uncomfortable and won't be let off easy with pat or myopic answers. You'll be pulled time and again into the path of the Spirit speaking through Scripture. And you will be better for it."

BARNABAS PIPER, Podcaster; Author, *Hoping for Happiness*; Director for Community, Immanuel Church, Nashville, TN

"One of the more important skills for the 21st century is learning how to hold our theological convictions without giving in to divisive controversy. The body of Christ is so much more than the sum of its divisions, and Adam Mabry has given us wise guidance on how to maintain unity and disagree agreeably when it comes to complex theological topics."

TIM MACKIE, Co-founder, The Bible Project

"Provocative, refreshing, and compelling reading. This book will expose unhelpful and unnecessary divisions, and enable healthy, gospel-empowering unity. A must-read for staff teams, lay leaders, and any thinking Christian."

PAUL DALE, Senior Pastor, Church by the Bridge, Sydney, Australia

"In the age of social media, it has become easier than ever to share opinions (informed or not) without considering how they may affect others. In light of our mandate to make disciples, it is vital that Christians understand how and when to engage one another (and the world) in truthful and gracious conversation. Adam's book offers significant wisdom and points us back to what really matters. My suggestion: buy this book, read it, and stop taking sides."

STEVE MURRELL, President and Co-founder, Every Nation Churches; Founding Pastor, Victory Philippines

"Challenging, stretching and in some places quite uncomfortable. Adam challenges us to grow in humility towards Scripture and other Christians, especially those who understand things differently to us."

LINDA ALLCOCK, The Globe Church, London; Author, *Deeper Still*

"A book for such a time as this. *Stop Taking Sides* is incredibly balanced in its ability to remain rooted in the gospel and challenge its readers to manage tension. It is laced with wisdom and insight for now and for future generations. I couldn't endorse this book more."

ADRIAN CRAWFORD, Pastor, Engage Church, Tallahassee; CEO, GameSpeed Skills

"Someone has said that Christians are porcupines trying to hug each other. It's hard to fix without somebody getting hurt—and seriously. The remedy? It's Jesus and the Bible, of course—but it is also this book, which is about Jesus and the Bible. *Stop Taking Sides* is a practical, profound, and wonderful (though sometimes painful) book. Read it and give it to everybody you know. Jesus might change you—and the world. I wish every Christian would read this."

STEVE BROWN, Host of "Steve Brown, Etc."; Author, *Talk the Walk*; previously Professor of Practical Theology, RTS Orlando

"This book is so needed today! Our age has been called the information age, but it could equally be called the outrage age, the anxiety age, the fear age, or the tribalism age. Pastor Mabry has served us well by helping us see the necessity of embracing clarity, argumentation, listening, and mystery, as we seek to avoid these problems and live with a renewed mind and for the good of neighbor, Christian unity, and the advancement of Jesus' mission."

TONY MERIDA, Pastor for Preaching and Vision, Imago Dei Church, Raleigh, NC; The Gospel Coalition Council Member

"Thought-provoking, insightful, and biblical in describing the divine tension each of us navigates to be the light and influence God has called us to be in our generation. I highly recommend this book as one to put in your library to be read multiple times for maximum benefit!"

TOM LANE, Apostolic Senior Pastor, Gateway Church, Southlake, Texas

"An important word for followers of Jesus in our divided and polarized times. *Stop Taking Sides* offers a way forward and brings together qualities not often combined: it's both theologically robust and easy to read, both penetrating and witty, and both challenging and encouraging."

STEPHEN WITMER, Lead Pastor, Pepperell Christian Fellowship, MA; Author, *A Gospel in Small Places* and *Eternity Changes Everything*

"We all struggle to love our enemies. The true essence of love—to will the good of the other—requires strength of heart and mind. That strength is what Adam Mabry delivers in *Stop Taking Sides*. If you are ready to live the command to love, this book is the place to start."

ARTHUR C. BROOKS, Professor of Public Leadership, Harvard Kennedy School; NYT Bestselling Author, *The Road to Freedom*

"Adam skillfully applies to some of life's most perplexing conundrums this wisdom of Solomon: 'It is good to grasp the one and not let go of the other. The man who fears God will avoid all extremes' (Ecclesiastes 7 v 18). And he does this with a scholar's mind and a pastor's heart."

JIM LAFFOON, Global Overseer, Every Nation Churches

"This book could not be more timely. In a world of complexity where people love to take sides, this book offers a thought-provoking, challenging, and surprisingly refreshing alternative.

JOSH KIMES, Pastor, Hillsong Boston

"This is the book Christians need right now, in a world where people are only too happy to divide and cancel one another. As you read this book, you'll find many of your views confirmed, but also challenged. You'll be invited to avoid simplistic answers of one, the other, or an unthinking average. Instead, you'll feel the invitation to hold to all of Scripture."

JOSEPH BONIFACIO, Director, Every Nation Campus, Philippines; Lead Pastor, Victory Katipunan

"Excellent for Christians seeking to be faithful to Scripture who are frustrated by an age marked by truth abandonment and narrow tribalism."

TOM JACKSON, Senior Pastor, CentrePoint Churches, Scotland; Professor of Theology, Every Nation Seminary

"Adam brilliantly navigates today's biblical and cultural tensions that are too often downplayed or tossed to the wayside. For it's not just my way, your way, or the highway. There's actually another way that Adam masterfully sets out in the pages of this book. Don't miss it!"

DANIEL IM, Pastor; Podcaster; Author

STOP TAKING SIDES

How Holding
Truths in Tension

Saves Us From
Anxiety and Outrage

ADAM MABRY

Stop Taking Sides
© 2020 Adam Mabry

Published by:
The Good Book Company

thegoodbook.com | thegoodbook.co.uk
thegoodbook.com.au | thegoodbook.co.nz | thegoodbook.co.in

ISBN: 9781784984465 | Printed in the UK

Design by André Parker

CONTENTS

INTRODUCTION

"**Y**ou can't let those people think that they could have voted for Donald Trump and actually be Christians!"

I preach with an edge, but I rarely get yelled at afterward. But, firm in her conviction, she planted herself before me as I stepped off the platform, ready to fight for her side. In my sermon, I had made the point that Christians cannot hate each other, especially over politics. My mistake (in her eyes) was to invoke the 2016 US presidential elections and the derision some Christians lobbed at "those people" who had supported the other side (and how "those people" promptly returned the favor). Apparently, I should have taken her side—the "correct" side.

I tried to explain that Christian love meant loving all the people Jesus bled for, even when they held different political beliefs than we wished they would. After five minutes of my best pastor-voice, she thought silently, and then concluded, "Fine, but you can't let them think what they did is ok."

At this point I politely excused myself and headed out the door. The cool New England air greeted me as I walked to the car. Settling into automotive obscurity, I did what many humans now do instinctively—I checked my phone. An email popped up. It was from another Christian who'd heard my sermon, denouncing my approach as taking it too easy on "the lefties." He informed me that he'd now be looking round for another church—one that was on the "correct" side.

I was silent.

Then—unexpectedly—I laughed.

Perhaps it was the absurdity of getting opposite complaints about the same sermon that made me laugh. Perhaps it was the irony of my main point having been missed entirely, and the approach I'd been preaching against being embodied so perfectly. But I think that mainly my laughter was covering a deep sadness I felt—and still feel—over our tendency as Christians to anathematize each other over so many things.

WHEN SAINTS TAKE SIDES

I'm a pastor in Boston, Massachusetts. Pastoring in the educational hub of the world is great. But less great is the close correlation between perceived intelligence and strongly-held opinion. The "smart" folk in the media no longer treat disagreement as an occasion for conversation but for tribal competition, mud-slinging, and point-scoring—and five minutes on any social-media platform will show even the most optimistic of us that the world takes its lead from its media. In their *Hidden Tribes* study, More in Common—an international initiative trying to understand this phenomenon—found that "many of today's most contentious issues are framed as us-versus-them identity-based struggles."[1]

Technology isn't helping either. Silicon Valley promised us an advent of peace through constant digital connection. But

---

1 *The Hidden Tribes of America* (https://hiddentribes.us/pdf/hidden_tribes_report.pdf, accessed 4.20.20), page 70.

what we got was mostly a repository of porn, distraction, and cat videos, and a lot of tribalization. Ghettoized by giant tech companies into digital alleyways, we increasingly find ourselves in an echo-chamber of the like-minded, close enough to the next tribe to lob hateful comments but far enough from them to make engagement, love, and thought near impossible. The result? Side-taking, and a lot of it.

In the second decade of the third millennium, this is how the Western world works (or doesn't). And sadly, so does the church. We, too, are very, very good at setting up tribes, drawing boundaries, and looking down on those who are on the "wrong side." We're so much better at knowing what we are not, and why "they" are wrong, than we are at listening closely, loving deeply, and being willing to learn from the other. In some ways, we're even worse than the world: we rage about the same things as the world (politics, anyone?) and then, when we're done arguing over those things, we heap theological tribalism on top, just for good measure.

And so the church—Christians, including you and me— misses out on the unity Christ prayed for, on the experience of life Christ died and rose for, and the compelling witness that Christ called for.

Don't you wish there was another way? Aren't you exhausted by the constant arguing? Don't you wish we'd all start listening, and that Christian spaces, be they physical or virtual, could feel more like heaven than hell? Does it concern you what tribalism is doing to our witness? Do you worry that the "others" may have a point and you're missing out on something God is offering you, but you daren't put your head over the parapet of your team's trench and make that point?

If you wish this, or worry about this, then the antidote is disarmingly simple: Stop Taking Sides.

TRUTH IS TRUTH, AND SOMETIMES IT'S BINARY

First, I want to be clear about what I'm not saying.

I'm not saying Christians should never take sides. To be a Christian is to take that side, and to therefore not be a thousand other things. The Christian journey begins with repentance—a literal turning away from sin and toward salvation. Christianity is founded on truths that require turning from the "side" of non-truth:

- God is God: Everywhere, the Scriptures affirm that God exists, and there is no God like him.

- God creates: Everywhere the Scriptures affirm that God made the world and made us.

- Jesus is Lord: There's no debate over the lordship of Christ. He's the Savior, and he's the boss. This glorious fact stuns us and saves us, if we confess with trusting hearts (Romans 10 v 9).

- We are saved by faith and not works: While the Bible cares deeply about what we do, Scripture is clear that salvation comes through trusting God's promise to save in Christ, not by any other means.

The above list is not exhaustive, of course. But it demonstrates that the method of taking the Bible more seriously, not less, means that we take our stand on certain doctrines.

But... the fact that our faith contains some key binaries doesn't mean that everything in our faith is similarly binary. Not everything is a hill upon which to die. There are certainly moments when we must echo Martin Luther's "Here I stand, I can do no other"—but there are simply far more moments when we must think harder, pray longer, and draw closer, especially to those with whom we disagree. Not all who disagree with us are heretics. In fact, they probably have wisdom we should hear and maybe even a position we should embrace.

Second, I'm not calling for balance, where you try to hold all things as true at once. Truth cannot be balanced with lies. Jesus didn't "balance" Judaism with Roman paganism, nor did Paul or Peter, who followed him.

Third, I'm not talking about some Aristotelian middle way, choosing the best of what both "sides" have to offer and creating our own path. That's just the road to autonomy, and away from biblical authority.

Fourth, I'm not talking about saying that everyone's right and it doesn't really matter what you think as long as it works for you. A bloody cross—an act of divine disagreement with the way humanity had ruled itself—was the work of a Savior who died precisely because there are matters that matter. "Agreeing to disagree" is often just a mask for pride (they're wrong, but I can't be bothered to show them that they are) or for laziness (who knows who's right, but I can't be bothered to work it out).

HOLDING THE TENSION

To stop taking sides we must start to see. So, here's what I offer: a way for you to see where you're taking sides that the Scripture doesn't call you to (in fact, it calls you not to) and instead to start holding truths in tension: that is, to let the Bible tell us sometimes that two truths are both-and rather than either-or, and we need to live and grow in the tension of believing and holding to both. To stop sublimating some biblical teachings to others that we prefer, and to start listening to how the Bible is teaching. Here's why I want to offer it: because holding truth in tension not only brings us more into line with God's word, but it frees us from the anxiety and outrage that threaten to destroy us. Taking sides and throwing stones steals joy and decimates virtue. So this book offers you nine pairs of truths that represent some of the ground on which we are most prone to plant a flag, see the terrain as "either-or," and fight the "others." Embrace the tension and you'll grow in virtue, and gain a fuller experience of the Christian life.

If, like me, you often feel tempted to take sides, take heart. In a world of complexity, we all long for simple answers to hard questions. Like me, you probably feel a lot of pressure to choose your team—to be *either* this *or* that— and it's difficult to resist the herd impulse. Resisting that urge to take sides is difficult, and downright humbling. But that's part of the point. It takes virtue to state doctrines clearly, and virtue to hold them in tension when Scripture does. Virtue is hard, but nothing truly worth having is easy. Everything good is hard, and virtue is no exception. But, if we'll take the Bible more seriously, we may start to be known not for what we're against, but for an attractive virtuousness.

BEFORE WE BEGIN

Before we start this journey, it's worth reflecting on the location of our beginning. This simple graphic illustrates what I mean:

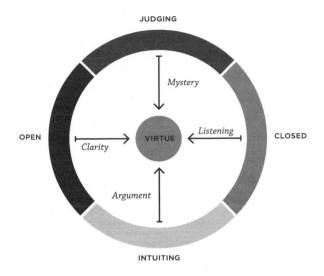

We're all on this circle somewhere, so locating ourselves will help us know what it will take to move forward. No one of the starting points is better than another—each has its strengths and weaknesses. But if you find yourself seeing only your strengths and the weaknesses on the other "side"—well, please stop taking sides.

"Openness" refers to your degree of acceptance of the new and the other, while "Closedness" describes your degree of firm conviction about truth and morality. "Intuiting" describes your degree of reliance on the promptings of the Spirit, wisdom, and an inner leading, while "Judging" describes your degree of reliance on sound reasoning, facts, and rules.

Take a moment and ask yourself, "Where do I tend to sit?" (Maybe ask someone who knows you well, too.) You can even draw a dot on that map (go ahead, I don't mind). My point here is simple: that where we start isn't where we should stay. Virtue lies in not letting go of the strengths of where we begin, but holding our strengths honestly in tension with the strengths of what we are naturally not. Jesus, of course, is our goal. He was the perfect embodiment of all these four qualities, which is why Christ-like virtue is found as we move sanctifyingly toward other strengths—toward him.

If you're naturally high in openness, you need to remember the Bible speaks clearly. It's not changing; it's not wrong. And that fact of doctrinal clarity must constantly rebuke and reward you. For the feeling-based intuiters, the challenge is to stop only thinking with your feelings, and let logic and sound arguments speak to you. I don't mean "arguments" as fighting but as substantive reasoning and the careful articulation of truth. Facts aren't feelings, and the Spirit wrote a book that makes sense. If you're closed, listening is going to be necessary—especially listening to the more open among us or those who aren't already saying what you want to hear, remembering that they often have a point and a helpful perspective. And finally, if you're more judging, then you like your lines nice and neat, and your doctrine all sewn up—so you'll need to consciously, willingly embrace paradox and mystery. For, while God knows all things, you don't, and you can't. You must learn to trust him, not your ability to understand him.

Clarity, argumentation, listening, and mystery—these are the tools that will enable us to stop taking sides, embrace tensions, and for God's sake be free from constant fear, proud tribalism, and sprawling anxiety. "How beautiful are the feet of them who publish peace," wrote Isaiah, during his own difficult cultural moment. If we'll embrace biblical tensions, we'll experience virtue's beauty.

So, let's dive into the first tension: sovereignty and responsibility.

1. SOVEREIGNTY *AND* RESPONSIBILITY

"He is not a tame lion."
Mr. Tumnus, from *The Lion, the Witch, and the Wardrobe*

"It's our choices, Harry, that show who we truly are..."
Dumbledore, from *Harry Potter and the*
Chamber of Secrets

"It's called predestination."

It was a hot July afternoon, and 14-year-old me was headed back home from summer camp with the church youth group. A new kid was waxing philosophical, using words like "sovereign" and "election"—words I had not encountered. I barely understood what he was saying. A few rows back on the bus, I was only half-listening. But, when he uttered that word—*predestination*—I sat up. I didn't know what he meant, but I knew I didn't like it. Was this guy suggesting that God chooses some people but not others?

Maybe it was the heat at the back of the van, beyond the air conditioner's reach. Maybe it was the friction of strange ideas abrading my own. Or maybe it was just the fear of encountering concepts I wasn't sure of. Whatever the reason, I loosed off my entire arsenal of biblical argumentation against this offensive idea (which, as I had only been a Christian for a few years, took mere minutes). From a few rows forward my new not-friend pushed back, and before long things got heated, so we thought it best to let the conversation break off. But a few weeks later, he handed me a copy of John Piper's *Desiring God*. "Read this," he said. "Then, let's talk." Since he was older than me (which seemed very important at the time), I took the book, thanked him, and didn't read it.

The book sat forgotten on my shelf for months. I'd no intention of reading it, yet I was afraid to give it back. What was I to say? "Thanks for this. I didn't read it"? Eventually pride, peer pressure, or something else got the better of me, and I opened it up and started to read. It was akin to being judo flipped. I was offended to learn that this guy—a famous pastor-author—taught this idea. I was shocked to find out that Scripture appeared to support it. And then I hit a problem: the more I read, the more I realized that I might be wrong. Over time, my worry transformed into worship and my indignation into exaltation. I reread it. Then I re-reread it. Then I read J.I. Packer's *Knowing God*. Then R.C. Sproul's *The Holiness of God*. Then I did a Bible study through the book of Ephesians for a whole year. It kindled a deepening passion for this surprisingly sovereign God who I thought I had understood.

Being young and foolish, I now entered into the "cage stage" of theological awakening—where passion to share a newly discovered doctrine runs roughshod over love for others. So it was that the following summer, on another youth trip, there was another van scene and another "bite-off-more-than-we-can-chew" discussion about God.

But now I was the reformer, and now I was preaching the doctrines of grace with all the gracelessness of an inquisitor. I had texts. I had quotes. And I had a captive audience.

Arriving at our destination, I was surprised to discover that not everyone appreciated my doctrinal passion. Settling to bed, my roommates—my friends—seemed to be avoiding me. With the same boldness I had earlier showed, I asked why. They told me. I may have been right—they weren't sure and they admitted as much. But I wasn't loving—about that they were quite sure. One friend put it this way: "I don't know if you're right, Adam. But the way you're acting makes me want nothing to do with this idea, if this is what it turns you into."

They didn't feel they'd been near Jesus—just near a jerk.

TAKING RESPONSIBILITY WHEN TALKING SOVEREIGNTY

Conversations like this are too common. A brief scan of the comments section of a Christian website or a YouTube video will give you abundant proof that believing right doctrine—in this case, that God is sovereign over human affairs—is no guarantee of love. Knowledge puffs up (1 Corinthians 8 v 1), especially knowledge about God. Anyone who increases in knowledge risks arrogance—a risk multiplied when the subject is God. Of course, arrogance is not the wholly owned subsidiary of any theological position. It is, as we will soon see, a ubiquitous problem. My point in this chapter—if we have eyes to see—is that the tension in which the Bible sets the doctrine of God's sovereignty is the Bible's solution to this difficulty. The good news for us is that God loves neatniks, newcomers, and everyone who has ever been confused about how exactly to resolve the tension between God's sovereignty and human responsibility.

Resolving sovereignty and responsibility isn't my aim so much as showing how the Bible teaches us to *hold* this tension. The Bible teaches that God is in control *and* that our decisions matter. His will *will* be done, and he will hold us responsible for ours. God chooses his people, and we are responsible for trusting God. Many men far greater than me have theologized and philosophized about these biblical realities, drawing ever nearer to that horizon of mystery. I won't be doing that here. I'm here simply to say this: if we care more about being right about Jesus than following the way of Jesus, it won't matter that we're right about Jesus. I want you to see what took me so long to learn: the Bible's strategy isn't to explain God systematically but to confront us with truth in tension—to show us that paradox and mystery aren't bugs but features we must learn to lean into and not hide from. The Bible's teaching on sovereignty and responsibility is not an either-or truth tournament, nor an "emphasize one element and briefly acknowledge the other" discussion. It is a tension—one that requires bravery to embrace mystery. So, let's jump in and see just how Scripture does this when it comes to God's sovereignty and human responsibility.

COMPATIBLE AND CONFOUNDING

There are basically two sides to this debate about sovereignty and responsibility. One group (usually marked by the word "Reformed") celebrates the power, might, magnificence, and glory of God, highlighting Scriptures that sing, "Our God is in heaven, and he does all that he pleases" (Psalm 115 v 3). God leads human decision-making (Proverb 16 v 9). He declares "the end from the beginning and from ancient times things not yet done," accomplishing every single one of his plans (Isaiah 46 v 9-10). Because humans are dead in sin (Ephesians 2 v 1-3), we cannot choose God (because dead people don't make choices). So God chooses those who will be his own (John 15 v 16; Ephesians 1 v 5, 11), calling his chosen ones to himself when and how he pleases (Ephesians 1 v 3-6).

The other group (usually marked by the word "Arminian") is concerned to celebrate the dignity of human agency (Genesis 1 v 27), pointing out that God gave us a choice to follow him and that we failed in our responsibility (Genesis 3 v 1-7). In love, God created humanity with choice-making capacity, so it is up to us to "choose this day whom you will serve" (Joshua 24 v 15). By grace, this is how any Christian starts their lives in Christ, obeying his call to "repent and believe the gospel" (Mark 1 v 15). God "desires all people to be saved and to come to the knowledge of the truth" (1 Timothy 2 v 4), which means we are responsible for sharing this good news with as many others as we can, so that the whole world may know the God who desires to forgive them.

Notice all the Bible references that both "sides" can marshal. How do we resolve that? We don't, except to say that the Bible simply presupposes that both of these realities are true (as D.A. Carson notes in *How Long, O Lord?* [2]). Is God is absolutely sovereign, yet not in such a way that human responsibility is curtailed, minimized, or mitigated? Yes. Are humans morally responsible and rightly held accountable for their actions, but not in such a way as to make God's sovereignty subservient to their choices? Yes.

The tension is pretty obvious. How can God choose who will come to him (Ephesians 1 v 3-6) if he wants everyone

---

2   *How Long, O Lord?* (Baker Academic, 2006), page 201.

to come to him (1 Timothy 2 v 4)? How can God hold us responsible for our choices (Romans 2 v 16) if he's already ordained the future of his choice and knows everything that will happen (Isaiah 46 v 9-10)? These are good questions, which seem to only have "either-or" kinds of answers. Either God is running the show or we are. But not both.

Yet Scripture seems to say, "Not so."

Scripture *knows* that this tension exists, and it unashamedly presents it to us. God doesn't highlight his sovereignty in one book and then mention human responsibility in another. Nor does one author wax philosophical about human freedom while another comes along later to correct him. Extraordinarily, Scripture brings God's absolute sovereignty right up against inescapable creaturely responsibility. Let's look at four such places.

GOD CHOSE YOU, AND YOU CHOSE HIM

At various points, the Bible deeply offends our sensibilities. But for almost every 21st-century Westerner who bumps into it, the idea that God may have chosen certain individuals for special treatment sounds unfair at best and unconscionable at worst. But, if we approach Scripture with that conviction about any doctrine, we're not likely to be able to hear what Scripture is saying about any doctrine. That's the very definition of prejudice—to pre-judge before listening humbly to the evidence. God in Scripture cares less about preserving polite, Western sensibilities of fairness than he does about stunning us with the nature of his sovereignty. Space does not permit us here to catalog the hundreds of instances where the

Scriptures confront us in this way.[3] Instead, I want to zoom in on one of the many places where human responsiveness to the gospel and God's choice of those respondents is fused: Acts 13.[4]

> "The next Sabbath almost the whole city gathered to hear the word of the Lord. But when the Jews saw the crowds, they were filled with jealousy and began to contradict what was spoken by Paul, reviling him. And **Paul and Barnabas spoke out boldly** ... And when the Gentiles heard this, they began rejoicing and glorifying the word of the Lord, **and as many as were appointed to eternal life believed.** And the word of the Lord was spreading throughout the whole region ... And the disciples were filled with joy and with the Holy Spirit."
>
> (v 44-45, 48-49, 52, emphasis mine)

This passage, typical of many such accounts in Luke's second book, tells an exciting story about evangelistic success. Paul and Barnabas went into a city and preached the gospel; many responded with faith, and they were filled with joy. Paul and co. showed up, people got saved, the end. But that's not what Luke wrote, because the Spirit had something more for his readers to see.

Yes, Paul and Barnabas showed up. As they preached in synagogues and faced fierce opposition from the Jewish rulers, they called people to respond to the amazing news about Israel's true king. But Luke wants us to see that it wasn't merely their preaching that saved. Their preaching

---

3 For a such a rundown, see D.A. Carson, *Divine Sovereignty and Human Responsibility* (Wipf and Stock, 2002); Wayne Grudem, *Systematic Theology* (Zondervan, 1994).

4 This is a pattern in Luke's writing (see also Acts 16 v 14 and 18 v 10).

was made effective because "as many as were appointed to eternal life believed."

Many commentators have worked very hard to soften the force of this verse, but the whole point of this book is very much not to do that.[5] We are to take the Scripture as it comes to us and ask, "Why is the Bible knowingly doing this to us—forcing us to put two difficult-to-reconcile truths up against each other?" I would like to suggest that one reason is to foster in us the virtue of humility.

Without a verse like this, we might understandably conclude something like "Wow, Paul and Barnabas must have been amazing evangelists." If this were simply the story of human actions (evangelism) and human results (conversion and worship), then we would rightly admire and hope to imitate these men, or dolefully conclude that there's no way that we could. But this is not a simple story about humans; it's a window into the mysterious concept of election. So, the human stuff is interrupted by the shockingly brief point "and everyone who was appointed to eternal life believed." Without those words, we'd miss the formational point of this text—God chooses us, *and* we're responsible for choosing him (or not).

The clearest criteria we're ever given for God's electing choices are found in Ephesians 1. He chose his people out of love (1 v 4), for adoption (1 v 5), for the praising of his glorious grace (1 v 6). Not because we'd make useful members of his team, or we're the right fit, or we are somehow better than others—just because of pure, unmerited grace. Jesus himself affirmed these ideas all the time. See John 6 v 65-67, for example:

---

5   The Greek word, *tasso*, means "to designate, determine, or appoint."

"[Jesus said] 'No one can come to me unless it is granted him by the Father' [God chooses his people]. After this many of his disciples turned back and no longer walked with him. So Jesus said to the Twelve, 'Do you want to go away as well?' [People choose whether or not to follow God's Son]."

This is a counterintuitive teaching. The Bible clearly teaches that God chooses his people (time doesn't allow us to talk about his choice of Abram, Noah, the judges, Samuel, David, and so on), and the Bible clearly teaches that we are responsible for choosing to repent, believe, and obey. If I don't see how that fits together, that's ok. God is both different from and better than me, and that's good. (Mabry as God would not go well for the cosmos.) I am called to affirm both truths, and that will produce a humility in me that full understanding or camping out on one truth or the other never could.

100% GOD AND 100% YOU

We've seen that God saves his chosen people, and those people choose to trust God. Let's move on to the Christian life itself. Paul wrote Philippians 2 v 12-13 as an encouraging admonition. In a letter filled with gratitude, he writes:

"Therefore, my beloved, as you have always obeyed, so now, not only as in my presence but much more in my absence, work out your own salvation with fear and trembling, for it is God who works in you, both to will and to work for his good pleasure."

In the Spirit-inspired mind of Paul, no contradiction is involved in saying, *You Philippians need to get to work on understanding and living out the salvation Jesus gave you, because God is the one working in you so that you might will and work for him.* We want to ask, "But which is it, Paul? Is God working in me or I am working for him? Is it my will or God's will? Me or him, Paul?"

Frustratingly, yet freeingly, Paul's answer is "yes."

This text clearly teaches that we are 100% responsible to "work out our own salvation with fear and trembling," as we "will and ... work" for God's good pleasure. And, this text clearly teaches that God is 100% sovereignly at work "in you" so that you are enabled to "will and to work" for his good pleasure. So, who is making the willing and the working happen? God and you.

"But that's a contradiction!" we may say.

No, it's not. It's a tension. A contradiction would be something like "You are responsible and not responsible." Or "God is in control, but he's lost control." Logic is built on the bedrock of the law of *non*-contradiction, teaching us that a thing cannot be itself and its negation at the same time, under the same circumstances. That's why you've never seen a married bachelor or found the corner of a circle. The Bible never asks us to be illogical, believe contradictions, or say that lies are truths. Tensions, on the other hand, are ideas that *feel* as though they cannot be true at the same time, but are.

And the Christian life is found within this tension, not in running to the false security of your preferred side. Consider what happens if we don't embrace the tension of God's leading and our effort. If you think your growth as a disciple is all on God, you'll end up in a lawless "doesn't-matter-ism," since God will do whatever he wills. This has the veneer of piety, but it's tensionless pride or complacency.

But, if discipleship is all on you, you'll land in graceless "try-harder-ism," which will either make you proud of your religious performance or (if you're more honest) crushed by your failure to perform well enough.

Artificially resolving the tension contorts the text to teach something that either puts us in control—"I'm in charge of my own sanctification, so I'd better get to work"—or gives us an excuse—"God hasn't worked in me enough yet to desire not to sin, so it's not my fault." But humbly holding the tension helps us see the mystery of our sanctification. And in so doing, we actually become more sanctified.

GOD'S INTENTION IN EVIL PLANS

Joseph is one of the most popular figures of Old Testament history (somewhat because of his technicolor dream coat). But given the dysfunction of the rest of his family, it's probably fair to hold him up as an example to follow. We root for him all the way through his being sold into slavery, falsely accused of rape, cast into prison, and then completely forgotten. We cheer when he finally makes it, proving that God is with him and that he doesn't need his abusive brothers, and moving on to a new family. And we give a standing ovation when he lands the second most powerful job in the most powerful empire in the world of his time.

Then, in the middle of a devastating regional famine, weary travelers from beyond the borders of Egypt come to his court—his palace—begging to buy food. They look familiar... they *are* familiar. When Joseph realizes that these are his brothers—brothers who hated him, beat him, and sold him—his emotions erupt. He hatches a plan to teach them a lesson. Yet, somewhere along the way,

God seems to have worked on this favored son of Jacob, because when he finally reveals himself to his weary and worried brothers, tears of joy and forgiveness flow from them all.

Why was Joseph able to forgive instead of punish? Because he had embraced a beautiful biblical tension. When it was all said and done, here was his Spirit-inspired interpretation of events: "As for you," he said to his brothers, "you meant evil against me, but God meant it for good" (Genesis 50 v 20).

Joseph neither undermined his brothers' responsibility nor downplayed the immorality of their actions. "You meant evil against me." What they did was what they did, and what they did was evil.

And yet... God's intentionality was all over their actions. The warm rays of God's sovereignty shone even through and in the darkness of their evil actions. God "meant it" for good. God didn't just *use* it for good, *redeem* it for good or *allow* it for good. God's intentions were at work within their evil choice. He ruled over and in evil with a goal in mind. Imagine what would have happened had Joseph let go of this tension: that his brothers' actions were theirs, yet God was ruling and intending some good purpose even in those actions. If Joseph had denied their responsibility, he would have had no appreciation for God's grace in saving him from external evil. In fact, he may have even blamed God for it. Yet if he had reduced God's involvement, he would have reduced God's power and goodness to save even through the worst evil actions of others. The author of Genesis knew this. He was teaching us something about how God works for us even in the face of what seems like senseless evil. With

God, it's never senseless. Yet it's also never not evil. The author's aim wasn't to make systematic theology easier so we could "understand," but to set before us a tension so that we could be formed. His aim is to form us to be those who might humbly look for evidences of grace even in the greatest evil to form us—into those who humbly trust him even (and precisely) when we don't see how he is bringing about his good purposes. Holding the tension—difficult as it may be—will incubate humility.

JUST AS GOD PLANNED

When Peter preached the first Spirit-inspired Christian sermon at Pentecost, he told his listeners in Jerusalem that "this Jesus, delivered up according to the definite plan and foreknowledge of God, you crucified and killed by the hands of lawless men" (Acts 2 v 23).

If reading that verse didn't startle you, read it again.

This event in history—the worst crime ever perpetrated by humanity—was accomplished by lawless men *and* happened according to the unchanging, foreordained plan of God. God predestined an action that purchased our redemption, yet that action was the responsibility of sinful men.

God planned the evil, hateful, unjust murder of his Son. This is what is meant by John's description of Jesus in Revelation 13 v 8 as "the Lamb who was slain from the creation of the world" (NIV). The most pivotal moment in history is simultaneously attributed to a sovereign God and to lawless men.

Much is at stake here. Massage Scripture to say God simply worked some good from a not-good thing and you reduce the gospel to a mere happy accident. Contort Scripture to obliterate human agency and the line between

God and evil disappears, making God's word lie when it teaches that he bears no blame for evil (1 John 1 v 5), and making "he made me do it" a defense for every evil act. Twist it to exalt human agency and God is just a passive observer, frantically responding to whatever crazy choices we humans make.

So, instead of trying to resolve this tension, let's ruminate on it. Stare at this text for a moment. What do you see? A verse, in a book, among other books, all telling one, unified story. In that story, God is the author and humanity the characters. But this story is different from our stories in this important way: this Author hasn't just written a story; he stepped into it. Luke knew this when he wrote Acts. Inspired by the Spirit, he scripted out the precise words God wanted, yet they were his. So why these words in this way? Perhaps it was to surprise us with the way that God's sovereignty relates to human responsibility. Perhaps God wished to demonstrate just how answerable we are for our rebellion against his Son, even though this most awful moment of rebellion was part of his gracious plan to defeat that rebellion while rescuing us rebels.

FOR HUMILITY, HOLD THE TENSION

So, which side of the tension do you tend to be drawn to? Are you a "God's sovereignty" kind of believer or a "human responsibility" kind of follower? Do you build one truth up as a hill to die on while paying lip service to the other? Most of us take a side, whether by tradition, upbringing, or sheer preference. Holding the tension is—well, it's tense. You'll be tempted to tribalize. So, be careful. Preferring to brush duty under the rug of "Well, God is sovereign after all," you'll be inclined to shirk your moral responsibility. Equally,

"Free will demands that God's control be qualified" starts you down a road that often ends in exalting human liberty and increasingly diminishing God's supremacy. Eventually, he's just a bit-part player in your story: a shrunken God who simply watches what happens and "blesses it" when it makes him happy. We sacrifice much in an effort to understand how it all works.

And who ever promised that we would understand God's plans at all? If you and I demand comprehension as a condition of our submission, then virtue will ever elude us. The Bible invites us to know God but not to comprehend everything about him. Comprehension—complete understanding—is for math, physics, and the perfect chocolate-chip cookies recipe. Apprehension—looking at and enjoying something or someone—is for persons, relationships, and aesthetics. God's ways are higher (Isaiah 55 v 8-9); his plans are deeper (Romans 11 v 34). To demand full understanding of his choices is a fool's errand, like a toddler demanding to check his or her parents' taxes. From time to time God lets us in, explaining certain parts of his plan. But his explanations are not given that we might understand him but that we might adore him.

Two things can be true at once: God is far bigger than we know, and our decisions are more important than we imagine. We will never know the mind of the Lord. Not even a trillion years of traversing his mind in the kingdom to come will bring us to its end. Imagine the boredom of knowing a God you could master or match.

Good Bible readers observe what the Bible is doing *and* what it's saying. So, what is it doing? It seems like it's knowingly, intentionally presenting God's sovereignty and human responsibility *in a tension*. Over and over again, God's word does this. Which leads us to a second question: why?

Simply, God is more interested in forming my whole person than merely teaching my human mind. The adventure of apprenticeship under King Jesus isn't a systematic theology course; it's a sweat-and-blood slog through life with the Savior. This doesn't mean I don't value doctrine: personally, I've spent a lot of time and money getting degrees to understand it. But getting your doctrine right is not the same as growing as a disciple. When God confronts me with his sovereignty and my responsibility, I have a choice: resolve the tension by bringing doctrine down to the lowest common denominator of my comprehensibility, or grow in the virtue of humility.

So, what does it look like to hold the tension?

GOD SOVEREIGNLY WILLS YOUR VIRTUE AND RESPONSIBILITY

Here are a few ways that you can live in the tension, hone your humility, and hopefully fare better than I did back on the bus at those summer camps.

Admit Ignorance

Where Scripture is clear, we should be too. But where it's not, we venture mere guesses. Educated guesses? Maybe. Wise guesses? Possibly. But guesses nonetheless. The Bible doesn't tell me God's sovereign will in a particular tragedy. In a crime, God doesn't reveal the exact distribution of individual responsibility. So let's not pretend otherwise. Bravely declare the bold and the clear. We cling to the truth that God's providential purposes are always good; but, we are free humbly to admit our ignorance about God's specific purpose in a specific circumstance. "I know that what God's doing is good, but I don't know how right now" is usually wisdom. Guessing at anything deeper is often folly—drawing firm conclusions about anything deeper almost always is.

Accept Responsibility

God's sovereignty doesn't get rid of human responsibility; it grounds it. If God weren't keeping the chain of cause and effect connected, it would cease to exist. Decisions only lead to outcomes because God has decided that they shall continue to do so. So, embrace responsibility, strive for holiness, work for the goal of your heavenly calling, and serve the King with all your might. No excuses.

Worship Passionately

Incomprehension is a prerequisite of passionate praise. When your favorite sports star pulls off an amazing play and you don't know how they did it, you shout about it. When a musician executes a virtuoso line, you don't comprehend it, yet you greatly enjoy it. We praise and worship that which induces wonder. God's ways are higher than mine. Sometimes I can glimpse something he's done, in a way I would never have mapped out or imagined. Always I can look back to the cross to see the greatest thing he's done, in a way you and I would never have planned nor asked for. Comprehension is not a pre-requisite for wonder. So, in any circumstance, worship him passionately. His goodness is never in doubt, only our ability to comprehend his good plans.

God's sovereignty is no enemy of your responsibility. Your responsibility does not undermine his sovereignty. Live in the tension, and watch yourself grow in humility as you worship and obey our great God.

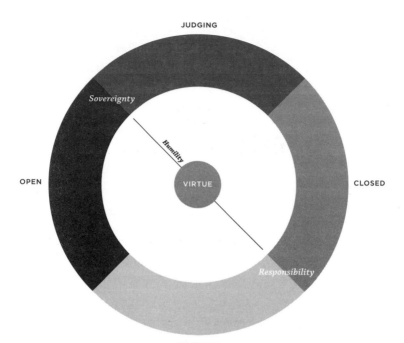

2. DIVINE IMAGERS
AND
DEEPLY FLAWED

*"On the whole human beings want to be good, but not too
good, and not quite all the time."*
George Orwell, *All Art Is Propaganda: Critical Essays*

*"The line separating good and evil passes not through
states, nor between classes, nor between political parties
either—but right through every human heart ... This line
shifts. And even within hearts overwhelmed by evil, one
small bridgehead of good is retained."*
Aleksandr Solzhenitsyn, *The Gulag Archipelago*

The restaurant business is a petri dish of human depravity.
From the age of eleven, I worked in restaurants.
(When your grandfather owns them, you're volun-told
to work in them.) Looking back, I can see that few jobs
prepared me more for full-time ministry than the decade
I spent serving food; but at the time, it was a mixed
experience at best.

One summer day I was waiting on a family of four.
Summers were busy in the beachside town where I grew
up. With two young children, it rapidly became obvious

that these parents practiced what we'll euphemistically call "free" parenting. They had had a day at the beach—evidenced by their sunburn—which had left them too tired to care too much about the behavior of their little ones. To them, our restaurant wasn't a place of business where people enjoyed food with their friends. It was a place to abdicate from the responsibility of parenting over a plate of seafood.

I took their orders, ignoring their kids. But when I came back from the kitchen, I found their son nosily wandering through the pass—the hall between kitchen and the dining room. During a rush, it was a dangerous place to be, with servers slinging food precariously balanced one-handed on trays. Advising mom and dad of this danger, I suggested that they keep an eye on their kid. Laughing me off, they assured me that their son was fine. He was "just tired" from a long day at the beach, and they'd get him in a minute. I went back to the kitchen to fetch and precariously balance some plates to another table.

With said plates loaded up and lifted up, I turned around and headed out the door. The next thing I remember was the crash. Plates were on the floor, food was everywhere, and my "just tired" little friend was crying. A lot.

Now free parenting gave way to the fully involved helicopter variety. Mom rushed in with theatrical compassion, weeping for "her baby." Meanwhile, dad rushed at me with it's-all-your-fault rage. Pointing out—with colorful adjectives—how I was to blame, he assured me that we'd hear from their lawyer. They stormed out without paying.

They didn't leave a tip, either.

OUR TWIN IMPULSES

Good and evil are entangled in the human condition, in a very everyday way. This entanglement was on display in that family. Good: a day at the beach followed by a family meal. Evil: unreasonable rage, refusal to pay, and sloppy parenting that abdicates responsibility because the kids are "just tired."

Good and *evil*?! Maybe you think that's a bit dramatic. "Evil" conjures images of Hitler and human tragedy. So why would we use it to describe a minor incident of slapdash parenting? Perhaps you're an optimist, inclined to think the best of humanity. After all, we have love, reason, compassion, and the invention of chocolate-chip cookies to our credit. We've built cities and invented air travel, medicines, and iPhones. This optimism is more or less the view of Steven Pinker, the cognitive psychologist and noted atheist. In his book *Enlightenment Now* he suggests that since the graph of our quality of life has been going up and to the right in the centuries since the Enlightenment, the dusty old doctrine of sin must be flawed. How could we be all that bad when we can do so much good?

Cue the pessimists. Citing the wars we fight, the waste we make, the abuses we hurl, and the wrongs we perpetuate, they, perhaps like you, are more disgusted by humanity than inspired. And when we think of holocausts, racism, selfishness, and the news cycle, the words of the nineteenth-century philosopher Friedrich Nietzsche start to sound more plausible:

> *"Once upon a time, in some out of the way corner of that universe which is dispersed into numberless twinkling solar systems, there was a star upon which clever beasts*

invented knowing. That was the most arrogant and mendacious minute of "world history," but nevertheless, it was only a minute. After nature had drawn a few breaths, the star cooled and congealed, and the clever beasts had to die. One might invent such a fable, and yet he still would not have adequately illustrated how miserable, how shadowy and transient, how aimless and arbitrary the human intellect looks within nature. There were eternities during which it did not exist. And when it is all over with the human intellect, nothing will have happened." [6]

Nietzsche wasn't much of an optimist.

But, who is right? Pinker or Nietzsche? We humans are confusing. On one hand, we're capable of amazing good; on the other, profound evil. We create families with cute babies, those aforementioned cookies, great art, pioneering science, and all sorts of wonderful things. But we also ruin families, abort babies, burn cookies, consume pornography, and live unhealthily, causing and experiencing indescribable pain.

So what in the world *are* we?

A BRIEF TOUR OF SOME BAD IDEAS

The "what are we" question has vexed civilization. At the risk of over-simplification, here are some abridged versions of the most common camps when it comes to understanding ourselves.

The Rationalists

Built on 18th-century Enlightenment ideals, this camp's sacred texts are those of evolutionary biology, physics, and

---

6 *Über Wahrheit und Lüge im außermoralischen Sinn* (1873), Part 1.

rationality. These science-minded secular priests usually say we're neither good nor evil because they deny that good and evil exist. Opting for phrases like "evolutionarily advantageous," they snicker at what old-fashioned types call morality. But this approach is filled with inconsistencies. If morality is just a trick of evolutionary biology, then how do we know that everything our minds tell us isn't similarly a trick? And why do we value love, beauty, and goodness?

The Romantics

That last question gave birth to this countermovement. Reacting to the Enlightenment, some balked at being reduced to mere biology. By exalting emotion, they waged war in the imagination. Where the Rationalists made laws and wrote philosophy, the Romantics made art and wrote plays. Sexually adventurous and morally ambiguous, they taught that humans had a prehistoric "state of nature," in which humans were born good. And if we're really good, then aren't our desires too? Yet, while it may initially be exhilarating to live this way, it is rife with problems. Feelings have no authority over facts, and facts frustratingly impinge on our desires all the time. For instance, there are no facts to support the theory that humans have an innocent "state of nature" at all—but there are many to suggest otherwise.

The Postmodernists

The Rationalists and Romantics fought their skirmishes for a century or two. But the Industrial Revolution, back-to-back world wars, the rise of Communism, and the Cold War gave birth to a new club—the Postmodernists. Fixated on power as the reserve currency of humanity, they sought to critique and demolish the other two camps, whom they blamed for the previous decades of tragedy. Today, Postmodernism is pervasive and has had the strange effect of creating secular demon-hunters who spend their days scouring films, politics, and social-media posts to exorcise the "devils" of privilege, power, and oppression. But like the camps it supplants, Postmodernism suffers from unlivable inconsistencies. If words are just tools that the powerful use for oppression, then so are the words of the Postmodernists. So why should we listen? And if "good" and "evil" are just tools of control, then so are words like "power" and "oppression." If everything is a power-play we should reject, why isn't Postmodernism?

GOOD GUYS OR BAD GUYS?

Despite their irrational inconsistencies, these camps exist because the question—*what in the world are we?*— is important. In fact, few beliefs are more important than those about ourselves. Your thoughts on you are the foundation of your sense of self-worth, morality, parenting, politics, and almost everything else. The good news is that we're not the first people to scratch our heads about ourselves. The ancients did, too, only differently— more through story than academic philosophy. They knew the power of stories to shape us.

For example, consider some ancient creation stories. In the case of Greek and Roman mythology, the origin story goes something like this: the gods fight chaos, win, and make humans to serve them. To take an example much more relevant to the story of the Bible, consider tales like *The Epic of Gilgamesh* from ancient Mesopotamia, or

Enuma Elish from ancient Babylon. To gravely oversimplify these epic tales, you'd likely walk away from reading them concluding that you were an inconsequential accident whose main purpose was to slavishly serve the gods. These stories, and others like them, were the bread-and-butter basics of the ancient world.

Turning to the Bible's story of beginnings, it's not hard to see plenty of literary parallels to those ancient myths. The "waters" of Genesis 1 v 2 don't refer to the substance in which fish live but to the chaos of an untamed world, just as the stories above reference chaos of one kind or another predating creation. But then the Bible's story quickly goes its own way, especially in these words:

> *"Then God said, 'Let us make man in our image, after our likeness. And let them have dominion' ... So God created man in his own image, in the image of God he created him; male and female he created them. And God blessed them. And God said to them, 'Be fruitful and multiply and fill the earth and subdue it, and have dominion' ... then the LORD God formed the man of dust from the ground and breathed into his nostrils the breath of life, and the man became a living creature."*
>
> *(Genesis 1 v 27-28; 2 v 7)*

Imagine living in the ancient Near East, sitting around a fire, the sky above you blazing with evening stars. Upon hearing *this* story, how would you feel? Shock. Wonder. For your whole life, you'd heard that the world was the outcome of cosmic conflict. Your social status was preset. Your innate value was small (unless you happened to be the king). Imagine the shock and surprise to find that in God's story, humans are handcrafted, God-breathed image-bearers. Wonderfully, unexpectedly, it turns out that you're neither an accident nor a slave. You're an intentional creation with a divine vocation. You are *imago dei*—made in the divine Ruler's image, to image him in making and ruling. Making families, gardens, homes, and whole civilizations is intrinsic to our God-like creation. We're not God, but we're *like* God, and that's something glorious. These ideas caused C.S. Lewis to write:

> *"It is a serious thing to live in a society of possible gods and goddesses, to remember that the dullest and most uninteresting person you talk to may one day be a creature which, if you saw it now, you would be strongly tempted to worship ... It is in the light of these overwhelming possibilities, it is with the awe and circumspection proper to them, that we should conduct all our dealings with one another, all friendships, all loves, all play, all politics. There are no ordinary people. You have never talked to a mere mortal. Nations, cultures, arts, civilization—these are mortal, and their life is to ours as the life of a gnat. But it is immortals whom we joke with, work with, marry..."* [7]

And then he spoils it:

> *"But it is immortals whom we joke with, work with, marry, snub, and exploit—immortal horrors or everlasting splendors."*

Immortal horrors or *everlasting splendors*?! Yes. Our creation story clearly states that humans are more amazing than most of us imagine. But it also tells us how we became capable of—and culpable for—more evil than we think.

---

7   *The Weight of Glory* (HarperOne, 2001), pages 45-46.

"Now the serpent was more crafty than any other beast of the field that the LORD *God had made. He said to the woman, 'Did God actually say, "You shall not eat of any tree in the garden"?' And the woman said to the serpent, 'We may eat of the fruit of the trees in the garden, but God said, "You shall not eat of the fruit of the tree that is in the midst of the garden, neither shall you touch it, lest you die."' But the serpent said to the woman, 'You will not surely die. For God knows that when you eat of it your eyes will be opened, and you will be like God, knowing good and evil.' So when the woman saw that the tree was good for food, and that it was a delight to the eyes, and that the tree was to be desired to make one wise, she took of its fruit and ate, and she also gave some to her husband who was with her, and he ate. Then the eyes of both were opened, and they knew that they were naked. And they sewed fig leaves together and made themselves loincloths." (Genesis 3 v 1–7)*

Imagine yourself in the ancient world again, sitting around the same fire, hearing these words. God made you with royal purpose—to carry his image in the way kings send forth viceroys. But in a twist of unexpected tragedy, these first human vice-regents became duped by another creature—an older, craftier one. Duped and deceived into believing that they were serving their self-interest, they agreed to serve him. Thinking they were achieving more freedom, they were shocked and saddened to discover they were defrauded, having sold themselves and their progeny into slavery.

This story is the origin of what theologians call "total depravity"—our total infection with sin. Every aspect of our image-bearing humanity—mind, will, body, soul, emotions, all of it—is now devastated by sin. By the first humans' disobedience, all humans are made sinners (Romans 5 v 18). Now we're not good or evil; we're good and evil. Nothing we do erases God's image in us, and nothing we do is untouched by our sinfulness. We each now live in the tension of *imago dei* and total depravity—a tension that every other origin-story misses, yet one which explains the data of human history.

GORDIAN KNOTS

The legend of the Gordian knot comes from the time of Alexander the Great. As the story goes, the Gordian knot was impossible to untie. Similarly, *imago dei* and total depravity are so entwined that we can't untie them either. Scholars have long discussed the meaning of *imago dei*. Some suggest that it's seen in our human rationality—the ability to string together a sentence, make deductions, and understand the world. In fact, the early Rationalists liked this very much. Others insist that *imago dei* is more about relationship and beauty. God, after all, is a beautiful Trinity, and we are made to be like him, capable of creating beauty and enjoying relationships too? That certainly sounds like something Romantics could support. More commonly today scholars see *imago dei* in our divine vocation of representing God and ruling under him. We have, according to Scripture, been given a divine command to bear fruit and tame the wild world (Genesis 1 v 28). The Postmodernist might be pleased to discover that the exercise of power is, in fact, part of the true human-origin story.

Each one of these angles on *imago dei* bears signs of truth. To greater or lesser degrees, rationality, relationships, and royal representation are helpful ways to understand how good humans are. But they also show us the devastation of total depravity.

We're made in God's image to think in the way he thinks. Yet sin corrupts our minds to such deep degrees that our reason is tainted by the irrationality of sin. For some it looks like distorted reasoning that oppresses or harms others. For others, it's irrational anger or irrational fear. Sin has caused our minds to work with a glitch. Bad thinking, mental illness, depression, anxiety... these are all echoes of depravity through the halls of our minds.

Relationships fare no better. In sin, the first humans hid, sewing fig leaves of false, shame-driven safety and identity. We're no different—our leaves just have more expensive labels. The beauty of relational intimacy is now scarred with hardship and hurt. Divorce, destruction of the family, division across lines of race, region, or wealth... these are all signs that our image-bearing has gone awry. Made in the image of a relational deity, we struggle in our relationships because of our intrinsic depravity.

And what of our call to rule and reproduce? Too often lust for power replaces the responsibility to rule. Some grow the bank balance or the business at the expense of the environment and other workers. Others just duck out of the responsibility all together. Why embrace such responsibility when video games and TV can simulate a less difficult reality? Why grow as a spouse when porn can deliver that desirable hit of dopamine? From crime to shoddy craftsmanship to the idolatry of career, instead of plumbing the rich depths of God's creation-ruling glory we often prefer splashing about in the shallows of our own greed and depravity.

This is the Gordian knot of human nature—you and me. Simultaneously, we bear the image of our Creator and the curse of our rebellion. Capable of great wonders and great woes, this is who we are.

But it is *not* who we will always be.

THE OTHER STORIES CAN'T EXPLAIN YOU

A hallmark of truth is its power to explain. Truth corresponds with the world as it is, not merely as we think it should be. This produces a virtue called prudence—seeing yourself and the world rightly. Without understanding humanity properly we cannot live prudently. The other stories can't fully explain humanity. Believing them, therefore, can only make us live wrongly, producing vice, diminishing human flourishing, and causing us to treat one another inappropriately. Ironically, the view that we are basically good is responsible for all kinds of evil—everything from the restaurant on that summer day to some of the most blood-stained battlefields of history.

The story of Rationalism is powerless to explain the things we find most important about life. Love, meaning, purpose, wisdom—these are nothing but useful fictions of evolution. Humanity just needs tinkering with, and eventually we'll arrive in Utopia. If all we are can be explained by molecular biology, we can evolve our way to the good life, right? But history is scarred by the vice of such optimists. The dictators who killed millions to speed evolution along were all, one way or another, utopians. One of the most frightening aspects of the Holocaust, the Soviet gulags, and the Chinese Cultural Revolution was how reasonable they seemed to so many. Concentration camps, gulags, political prisons—these don't seem like Elysium. Heaven seems to always be just around the corner when this story rules—and meanwhile, hell seems to make frequent appearances.

Romanticism struggles just as much. If we're all just blank slates and our natural state is best, why does it end with so much devastation? Following our passions and desires won't bring about a better world because doing so denies the reality of human sin. Far from prudence, this can only produce hedonism—the pursuit of pleasure as the ultimate good, at the cost of anyone who gets in the way. For any who have tried that way of life, it starts off really well. Sex, drink, food, and success are fun—for a while, at least. But the law of diminishing returns soon kicks in, and more food, drink, sex, or money is required just to get to the same high—the same payoff as the first taste gave. Romantics are stuck in a Sisyphean hell of seeking to match their first pleasure, yet condemned to never find satisfaction. Often too late, Romantics find themselves sick, broke, and alone. That blank slate is broken.

Postmodernism, though, may be the worst of all. Power just doesn't explain how the world actually works. Just maybe it explains politics; but parenting, not so much. Deconstructing all ideas down to cynical plays for power deconstructs you, too. For all your own ideas must be that way as well. This can only lead to nihilism—a sad meaninglessness that maroons you in the only place cynicism can lead to: you, with no meaning, untrusting, and alone. Postmodernism kills with the freedom it offers—like an astronaut floating untethered in endless space, or a diver forever sinking in bottomless water. If that's not hell, I don't know what is.

In the end, every story that denies either *imago dei* or depravity (or both) attempts to reduce humans to just one kind of thing, be it power, pleasure, pure reason, or something else. But this reductionist tendency can't dissolve good and evil. It always has to plant its flag in one or the other—and then watch as humanity stubbornly refuses to conform as the program that either assumes we are essentially good or that ignores the truth that we are capable of good doesn't work. Take the view that we're basically good and you'll be perpetually surprised and disappointed. Take the view that we're just awful and you'll never notice the beauty and goodness around you and inside you.

So let's turn our attention back to the only story that resolves the tension.

TENSION RESOLVED

Jesus was born a real flesh-and-blood human. But, born of a virgin, he was more than a mere human. His life was lived sinlessly, according to humanity's original design. His reason functioned perfectly, without the tarnish of sin. His untainted teaching showed us what God is like and what we are like, perfectly. Regaining the rule that Adam gave away, he rightly represented God, as we were made to but fail to do. He, the image of the invisible God (Colossians 1 v 15), represented him to our rebellious race. And we killed him. He was not tarnished by depravity, but he was subjected to it. And he underwent that death so that our relationship with God and other humans could have a happier ending. For Jesus didn't just die, trading his perfect humanity for our total depravity. He also rose, *imago dei* eternally, obtaining the victory. With flesh that will never die again, he promises that he will come back again. And when he comes with his kingdom, we who have trusted this King will rise too—with bodies *like* his into a new world *of* his. One day, the humans you meet won't be a tragic tangle of God's goodness and sin's brokenness. Our depravity will be a memory. The Gordian knot will be untied.

One day, but not yet. So for now, we have to hold the tension. Are we good? Yes. Are we evil? Yes. Only by seeing yourself and others this way will you gain the prudence to live well and wisely—and to love well and wisely.

Prudence Demands That We Hope in Christ

We must have hope. The world that the Father promised, the Son purchased, and the Spirit is ushering in is the best of all possible worlds. When human depravity looms large in your view, remember *imago dei*, and that through Christ goodness will one day win. Never place your hope in a program to fix humanity. Neither Marxist utopias nor social-justice schemes, neither physical pleasure nor the invisible hand of the free market can produce a new humanity. Christ alone is worth your hope, because only Christ can recreate humanity.

Prudence Reminds Us That There's a Struggle

There is a battle within every Christian: between the Spirit turning us toward God on the one side, and our sinful condition which is still in love with our depravity on the other (Galatians 5 v 17). If we're going to live lives more influenced by our born-again power than our first-born nature, we must rely daily on the Holy Spirit. Paul admonished the Ephesians to "be being filled with the Holy Spirit" (Ephesians 5 v 18, author's translation). That's good advice for your daily fight against your depravity. Sinful nature in its death throes is a dangerous opponent. We need God's Spirit for power and fruitfulness. The more of him we receive, the better we will see and the more we will become our true selves.

Prudence Requires Us to See Humans Rightly
We're a tragic mix of *imago dei* and total depravity. Holding this tension rescues you from utopianism and hedonism, nihilism and cynicism. If you want to treat humans well, you must understand what we humans are. And what we are all, right now, is a mashup of these twin natures. The best person you know is a seat of depravity. The worst person you know is an image-bearer of our Creator.

Prudence Obliterates the Pursuit of the Perfect Spouse
The hunt for Mr. Right becomes a complete waste of time when this tension takes root in your soul. Why? Because there's only one Mr. Right, and we worship him. The rest of us are, at best, Mr. and Ms. Might-be-right-for-me. There's no perfect man to marry, and no wife who will complete you. The person you wed is frustratingly and wonderfully human. If you forget that your spouse is a sinner, you'll be shocked, surprised, and crushed by his or her humanity, and you'll react with anger—growing distant or simply walking away. If you forget that your spouse is an image-bearer, you won't hope for them, pray for them, or serve them. And, reacting with antipathy, you might leave, just to go back on the hunt for Mr. or Ms. Right(er).

Prudence Helps You Parent Well
Helicopter parents are convinced that only by carefully and exquisitely curating every detail of their children's lives will they become happy, healthy adults. They are neo-Rationalists, hoping to create a little utopia through organic eating, safe living, seatbelt wearing, and constantly communicating. Free-range parents reject this, convinced that most people are good—especially their people. They are neo-Romantics,

hoping to raise good adults by not really raising them much at all. But the truth is that our children are depraved little image-bearers—wonderful and sinful. And knowing this will rescue your parenting. As you remember that Jonny bears the image of God, you'll help him develop his own image-bearing by pulling back on your over-controlling tendencies. And as you remember that he and others are sinful, you'll keep him from following others into evil or leading himself into it, pointing him to the Savior who can save him. Able to enjoy the good in your child and to see the sin in them, you'll prudently raise them, neither crushed by your inability to perfect them nor puffed up and blinkered by a glossy-eyed view of them.

Prudence Overhauls Our Political Ideologies
We'll look more at politics later. For now, it's worth realizing that Christless conservatism and godless progressivism have this in common: they are selling a salvation story that we must stop buying. When you realize that all humans are image-bearers, it makes certain policies unthinkable. Abortion, racial stratification, selfish wars, and the abuse of power are impossible to justify if all humans bear the image of God. Likewise, lax law enforcement, over-promising and therefore over-funded educational initiatives, and the endless expansion of the state are impossible to justify if all humans are vexed by sin. Unjustified humans can never construct truly just systems, and unsaved humans can never be saved by the state. Holding these truths in tension, we'll hold our ideologies with wise suspicion, and subservient to our gospel confession—not the other way around.

The truth in the tension between *imago dei* and total depravity goes a long way for me. It helps me understand that day at the restaurant years ago, that fight with my wife a few weeks ago, and that evil thought just a moment ago. It helps me love humanity, and humans individually, all the while aware of our collective depravity. Learning to hold these twin ideas will do wonders for you too. It's tough to live with this tension, but it's worse when we don't. The arms of Christ were stretched out wide so this tension could be resolved. So maybe we should open our arms to others, armed with the prudent knowledge of what they are, and the glorious potential of what they one day could be.

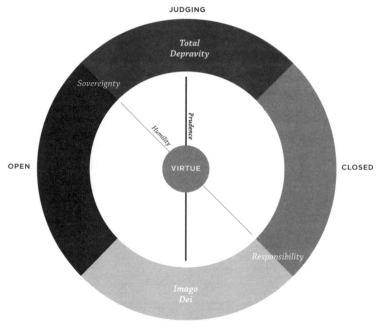

3. WORD
AND SPIRIT
AND TRADITION

"When the Scripture speaks, God speaks."
Martin Luther

*"I cannot imagine how religious persons can live satisfied
without the practice of the presence of God."*
Brother Lawrence, *The Practice of the Presence of God*

Mr. Zimmerman wasn't your typical white-haired Presbyterian attorney. Most elderly attorneys don't have a teenage fanclub. Then again, most of them don't welcome dozens of teens into their home each week. But Mr. Zimmerman did. Most them probably wouldn't tolerate the movie-watching, the music-playing, and the serial-snacking mess we left behind. But he did.

As a friend of his daughter, I came to his house at her invitation. I kept coming back because each of these weekly gatherings culminated in a fascinating Bible study (and because of the cute girl I met there who is now my wife, but that's a different story). Week by week, verse by verse, he guided us through the book of Ephesians over the course of a year. I'd never read the Bible like that, and his love for the text kept me coming back.

Equally, Pastor Jim wasn't your typical pastor. Most pastors don't travel the world, but he did. Most of them don't tell firsthand accounts of miracles, but he did. And most of them don't talk about the Spirit like he did. Like Mr. Zimmerman, Pastor Jim was older, wise, and godly, with a deep love for Scripture. But Pastor Jim had his own set of gifts. He would pray for people, and the things he prayed for would happen. He would speak to people and say things about them that no one else knew. As I got to know him, I came to understand that these were spiritual gifts. I'd never experienced the presence of the Spirit like that, but his love for God's Spirit kept me coming back.

These two men—one a Reformed Presbyterian elder, the other a charismatic, prophetic teacher—personify two worlds that I have come to occupy. I'm what is called a Reformed charismatic. I'm Reformed: deeply shaped by men like Martin Luther and John Calvin, with a love for Scripture and the message of salvation by grace alone, through faith alone, in Christ alone, for the glory of God alone. Yet I'm also rooted in the Spirit-filled movement of global Christians that has come to be called "charismatic" after the Greek word *charismata*, (the New Testament word for "grace gifts"). I admire the missionary zeal of believers in the global South and East along with the spiritual power and miracle-producing faith they embody.

I love the word of God, and I love the Spirit of God.

That's a tension.

In fact, these days, that's a provocation.

WORD OR SPIRIT?

Since I met those men and then entered full-time ministry myself, the dynamic tension of word and Spirit has animated almost everything I've done. It has colored my approach to academic research, shaped the way I pastor my church, and changed our whole approach to discipleship. It's a tension I'm convinced is wholly biblical, fruitful, and compelling; yet it's one that is difficult to manage, depending on your theological tribe.

Not without controversy, the arrival of Pentecostalism and its follow-on, the modern charismatic movement, rocked the global church. Most historians locate the official start date of this movement as April 9, 1906, when a young black preacher named William Seymour led a revival meeting at 312 Azusa Street, Los Angeles. Quite unexpectedly, attendees reported receiving the gifts of tongues, prophecy, and miraculous healing. The news spread like wildfire, causing a revival meeting to last for years. Since then, this upstart movement has grown to 700+ million such Christians, making it the fastest growing segment of the church, which is unparalleled in the history of missions.[8] Of course, just because something grows quickly that doesn't mean it's healthy. Revivals grow quickly, but so does cancer. And this movement hasn't been without its malignancies. Suspicious that this movement seeks to up-end biblical authority, some decry its perceived excesses.[9] Exuberant at the fruit of conversion, others celebrate its power in missions. Now, you may be reading

---

8 Allan Anderson, "Global Pentecostalism," a paper presented at the Wheaton Theology Conference, 3 April 2015, Wheaton College, Wheaton, IL.

9 Most notable among those are books like *Charismatic Chaos* by John MacArthur (Zondervan Academic, 1993).

through this paragraph full of concern or full of excitement. But the tension is unarguable.

That tension didn't appear in 1906 but at Pentecost. Since then, the relationship between God's unchanging, authoritative word and God's dynamic, wind-like Spirit has been a challenge to hold faithfully. The apostles had to deal with the Spirit's work amongst the Gentiles alongside their understanding of the Scriptures (Acts 10 v 44 – 11 v 18; 15). The post-Acts church struggled to understand how to do ministry that was biblically faithful and spiritually powerful (see 1 Corinthians and Galatians). And the following generation did too.[10] If they all struggled, it shouldn't surprise us that we struggle too. And given our nature (as discussed in the previous chapter), it also shouldn't surprise us that the good fight to maintain this tension has frequently devolved into the not-so-good fight of theological tribalism. Down to our own day this argument rages, with whole denominations demanding that you put your flag down on one side or the other. This makes it unsafe to change your position and unthinkable to humbly hold this glorious tension. Each "side" has its vocal proponents, who are easily triggered to fight this tribal skirmish.

---

10 Examples abound, from Justin Martyr's *Dialogue with Trypho* to the Montanist Controversy. For more on this, and how ancient charismatic ministry relates to modern practice, see my publication, *The Function of the Charismata in Early and Modern Missions* at Reformed Theological Seminary (listed as *Missiological Necessity of the Charismata* at https://rts.edu/campuses/global/students/sample-student-theses/, accessed 4.20.20). Large sections of the *Didache*, the earliest post-Acts book of church order, are devoted to understanding and operating the gift of prophecy. Montanism, a second-century prophetic movement with a strict morality bears many similarities to recent Pentecostal Holiness movements. Although its leaders did not intend to undermine scriptural authority, the movement was nonetheless considered heretical by the emerging church authority.

SCRIPTURE, SPIRIT, & TRADITION

Based upon our preferences, upbringing, or geography, we tend to pitch up to a tribe that feels right. Some select churches for the Scriptural teaching, others for extraordinary spiritual experiences, and a few prefer the stability of tradition. This book is too short to do justice to each tribe's theology, but we can describe their centers of gravity.

Scripture (Study and Faithfulness)

The first center of gravity is that of the tribe of the Scriptures. This is the group that values Bible study and biblical fidelity. Most evangelicals sort themselves into this camp, along with some Lutherans and Reformed Christians. This tribe loves exegesis because they believe that's the best way to connect to the apostolic church and remain faithful today. And, since the Spirit wrote a book, Bible study — they suggest—is the best way to connect with him, too.

Spirit (Power and Presence)

The second center of gravity is that of the tribe of the Spirit. As a rule, they love the power and presence of God, and their worship patterns show that. This movement, in modern times, includes Charismatic and Pentecostal Christians. They practice spiritual gifts (see 1 Corinthians 12; 14; Romans 12) because they believe that's the best way to connect to the apostolic church and continue the mission. Since the Spirit wrote a book, it's probably best to listen to him when we read it.

Tradition (Wisdom and Historical Connectedness)

The third center of gravity is that of the tribe of tradition. With liturgies, vestments, and labyrinthine practices, this group includes (but is not limited to) Roman Catholics, Orthodox Christians, and some Anglicans. They love the wisdom of Christians past and staying connected to church history. The best way to connect with the apostolic tradition—they believe—is probably the apostolic succession. So when they are confused about word or Spirit or anything else, they consult tradition.

So, Scripture folk go to their conferences, sing hymns—none of that vapid, modern stuff—and talk theology. The sermon is the star and the bookstore is always humming. Spirit folk, meanwhile, go to Spirit-folk conferences, sing quite loudly, and talk miracles and prophecy. The worship is intense and experience is the star. Traditional folk have conferences too. With pastors in collars, liturgy is the star, and conversations abound about favorite church fathers.

And all of us are united in looking down somewhat at the others. Among my Spirit-loving, loud-singing pals, it is easy to feel disdain for the stereotype of the doctrinal neat-nick who doesn't care about people. With my Scripture-loving seminary friends, it's always tempting to burn the snake-handling, Pentecostal straw man. And my traditionalist friends find it hard not to shake their heads, thinking that both camps have lost their mooring to the historical church and are all the poorer for it. Of course, not everyone in every camp thinks or acts like this all the time. But in my experience it happens more often, and involves more of us, than we'd like to admit. So unlike the other tensions in this book, this is a trilemma—a tension pulled in three directions.

Why does this happen? It's because holding on to this tension, as we're about to see, is really quite hard. Let's look at the Bible, and discover the virtue within the Word-Spirit-tradition tension that we find there.

THE SPIRIT OF THE WORD

The Bible is a fascinating library of sixty-six books, written on three continents, by over 40 human authors, in all kinds of genres, in three languages, over a period of almost two millennia. Given such time, diversity, and geographic range, it's reasonable to ask, "How did that work?" The answer: the Spirit inspired it. But how? Perhaps you imagine a voice dictated Bible words to David, or controlled his hand as he wrote. Did Paul go into some kind of trance to write Philippians? No. The Holy Spirit simply inspired these authors to write what they wrote.

Inspiration is an important word. To us, the word sounds artistic—as in "This song inspires me" or "I don't feel motivated. I lack inspiration." But when we talk about how the Bible came to be, the word has a different and specific meaning. From the Latin *inspirare*, "to breathe into," it's connected to 2 Timothy 3 v 16: "All Scripture is God-breathed." That's the word *theopneustos*. *Theos* (God) and *pneuma* (breath/wind) means exactly what it sounds like— God the Spirit breathed the Bible, and he did so through the people who wrote it. It wasn't all dictated or beamed down from heaven. It was produced through a divine co-operation, as Peter explains: "For no prophecy was ever produced by the will of man, but men spoke from God as they were carried along by the Holy Spirit," (2 Peter 1 v 21). Let's unpack that:[11]

---

11   Obviously, I cannot go into a full-blown account here of how the Bible came together. A great book on the topic is Craig Blomberg's *Can We Still Trust the Bible: An Evangelical Engagement with Contemporary Questions* (Brazos Press, 2014).

- *Men spoke:* The Bible is a very human book of books. Peter sounds different than Paul. Isaiah reads differently than David. God didn't override the humanity of these men any more than he did the humanity of Jesus. The Bible is a human book about our human Savior.

- *From God:* While the Bible is a human book, it's not *merely* a human book. God is speaking through these poems, histories, letters, and Gospels. Forgetting that turns the Bible into a mythology book of wisdom or advice, letting us take or leave some parts over others.

- *By the Holy Spirit:* What the Spirit led the writers of Scripture to write was exactly what God wanted, and what they wanted too.

The word of God isn't only the word of God. The Bible is an intensely human book—it is the product of certain cultures, times, and languages. It's complex enough to satisfy the greatest minds, yet its message is clear enough to save the simplest heart. It is a glorious gift to God's people. But—and this must be stressed—if it is not a book inspired *by* the Spirit and understood *in* the Spirit, it is as useless for our salvation as the stone altars of our forebears. As the seventeenth-century theologian John Owen said, "Take away the work and powerful efficacy of the Holy Spirit from the administration of [the word], and it will prove but a dead letter, of no saving advantage to the souls of men."[12] And as we'll see, the Spirit's book says

---

12   *The Works of John Owen*, ed. William H. Goold, Vol 3 (T&T Clark), page 53.

a lot about the Spirit's role in the Spirit-filled people of Spirit-filled Jesus.

THE WORD OF THE SPIRIT

Because the Scriptures are the product of the Spirit, they're true. So, whatever they say about the Spirit is true as well. And they say quite a lot. The Word—the Son of God, who has come in the flesh (John 1 v 1-18)—came not merely to save us and take us to heaven, but to "in-Spirit" us and send us into the world (Acts 1 v 7-8). Jesus took on flesh so that all flesh could be filled with the Spirit. The Scriptures tell us that we've been found by God in order to be filled with God, and filled with God in order to be fruitful for God.

- Jesus promised that his church would be baptized in the Spirit: "He will baptize you with the Holy Spirit" (Mark 1 v 8).

- Jesus promised that in persecution "the Holy Spirit will teach you in that very hour what you ought to say" (Luke 12 v 12).

- Jesus promised that the Spirit would illuminate his teachings: "But the Helper, the Holy Spirit, whom the Father will send in my name, he will teach you all things and bring to your remembrance all that I have said to you" (John 14 v 26).

- Jesus commanded his disciples to "receive the Holy Spirit" (John 20 v 22).

- Jesus said his Spirit would give power to be his witnesses. "But you will receive power when the Holy Spirit has come upon you, and you will be my witnesses in Jerusalem and in all Judea and

Samaria, and to the end of the earth" (Acts 1 v 8). At Pentecost, Jesus sent his Spirit, and miracles broke out, "And they were all filled with the Holy Spirit and began to speak in other tongues as the Spirit gave them utterance" (Acts 2 v 4).

- Instructed by Jesus, Peter understood that the new-birth gift to the people of God was the Spirit of Christ: "Peter said to them, 'Repent and be baptized every one of you in the name of Jesus Christ for the forgiveness of your sins, and you will receive the gift of the Holy Spirit'" (Acts 2 v 38).

- Luke tells us that the same Christians who were there at Pentecost were again filled with the Spirit, enabling them to speak the word boldly. "And when they had prayed, the place in which they were gathered together was shaken, and they were all filled with the Holy Spirit and continued to speak the word of God with boldness" (Acts 4 v 31).

- The Gentiles received their own Pentecost, proving that the Spirit would be given to all Christians, and solidifying the understanding that anyone who believed the word of God in the gospel received the Spirit of God promised in that gospel. "While Peter was still saying these things, the Holy Spirit fell on all who heard the word. And the believers from among the circumcised who had come with Peter were amazed, because the gift of the Holy Spirit was poured out even on the Gentiles. For they were hearing them speaking in tongues and extolling God. Then Peter declared, 'Can anyone withhold water for baptizing these people, who have received the Holy Spirit just as we have?'" (Acts 10 v 44-47).

- Paul taught that Christians receive gifts from the Spirit: "Now there are varieties of gifts, but the same Spirit ... All these are empowered by one and the same Spirit, who apportions to each one individually as he wills" (1 Corinthians 12 v 4, 11).

- Ordinary Christians are commanded to eagerly desire the gifts of the Spirit: "Pursue love, and earnestly desire the spiritual gifts..." (1 Corinthians 14 v 1).

- We are commanded to be being (as in, over and over again) filled with the Spirit: "Do not get drunk with wine, for that is debauchery, but be filled with the Spirit" (Ephesians 5 v 18).

We should "be filled" with the Spirit—and not once, but in an ongoing, day-by-day manner. Jesus commanded his disciples to do exactly what Peter proclaimed at Pentecost—to receive the Spirit. What followed from obedience to these commands? Spiritual wonders like tongues, healings, and prophetic insight *and* the powerful proclamation of the word of God. The Spirit propelled the word, just as the word promised. So what happened post-Acts and beyond? To tradition—in the sense of the beautiful (albeit imperfect and sometimes confusing) story of church history—we'll now turn, briefly. After all, you and I know Jesus only because of millennia of faithfulness—teachers, preachers, mothers, fathers, intercessors, translators, and miracle workers, passing on the baton of the gospel. So let's consult them.

THE TENSION IN TRADITION

Tradition shows that the Spirit's work wasn't finished with the book of Acts and the completion of the canon, nor lost until Azusa Street. Spiritual power is not in competition with Scriptural fidelity. It is an attestation to it—not subversive but supportive. It's when we get this mixed up that the church drops the ball, because we've loosened our grip on either the text or the Spirit.

In Acts—which is the first book of church history—Luke very intentionally parallels the miracles of Peter, apostle to the Jews, and the miracles of Paul, apostle to the Gentiles.[13] Luke intended to overwhelm his readers with evidence that the Spirit's power is an irreplaceable aspect of God's strategy to advance the gospel.[14] This, our earliest tradition—and, as Scripture, divinely inspired—holds this tension with great diligence and great results. But in the century to follow, the tension would be tested.

The fall of Jerusalem to Roman armies in AD 70 marked the end of the apostolic age, leaving Christianity without its Jewish geographic center even as it spread further throughout the Roman empire and beyond its borders. During that time, the church was led by elders and teachers *and* by Spirit-empowered, prophetic ministers.[15] These

---

13 Compare, for instance, Acts 2 v 32, 27 and 14 v 3, 7; 3 v 1, 10-16 and 14 v 7, 21; 5 v 1-14 and 13 v 8-12; 4 v 31-37 and 16 v 25-31; 5 v 14-15 and 19 v 12, 20; 9 v 33-35 and 28 v 7-10; 12 v 5, 19 and 16 v 25-30. See also John Hardon, "The Miracle Narratives in the Acts of the Apostles," Catholic Biblical Quarterly, 16 (1996): 303-18.

14 An oft-repeated phrase in Acts is something like "the word of the Lord grew," noting the different stages of church growth into different parts of the world.

15 The *Didache*, an ancient book of church order dated to the first century, gives instruction to the church about how to treat these wandering prophets.

itinerant Spirit-empowered prophets did ministry alongside local teachers and were well known to the church fathers.[16] Justin Martyr, an early defender of the faith, wrote in his *Dialogue with Trypho* the best biblical and philosophical theology of his day. Within it, he said things like "Now it is possible to see among us women and men who possess gifts of the Spirit of God,"[17] and he told of exorcisms and healing in Jesus' name that he'd seen, and how these were happening "throughout the whole world."[18] For the first centuries after Acts, the Word-Spirit tension seemed to be holding.

The first real test came with the rise of the Montanists. The history of this group, named for their founder, reads like the wackiest of Christian TV. A guy (Montanus) who was known as a New Testament prophet gathered to his side two women (Prisca and Maximilla) who also claimed to be prophets. They began as orthodox Christians, but they made two big mistakes: (1) they elevated spiritual gifts over scriptural revelation, leading them to (2) teach errors—making prophetic claims that never happened, and teaching strict moral asceticism. The church reacted strongly, condemning them as heretics, even though some of our most important fathers were themselves Montanists (Tertullian, for example).

---

16 Historians have noted that two kinds of ministry emerged at this time: the apostles and teachers who taught the tradition of the church and the interpretation of Scripture, and the prophets who spoke from revelations they received directly from God. See Jerome Crowe, *From Jerusalem to Antioch: The Gospel Across Cultures* (The Liturgical Press, 1997); Ed Stetzer, "The Wandering Ecstatic Prophet in the Mission Strategy of the Early Church," Journal of Evangelism and Missions 1 (2003): 1.

17 "Dialogue with Trypho" in *The Ante-Nicene Fathers*, ed. Alexander Roberts and James Donaldson, Vol 1, (T&T, 1886), 6.1.

18 "Second Apology" in *The Ante-Nicene Fathers*, ed. Alexander Roberts and James Donaldson (T&T, 1886), 11.

Because the church sought to correct an imbalance with an overreaction, the gifts of the Spirit soon came to be viewed with suspicion. But the church had been led by prophetic ministers and local elders; so who would lead now? Politics, heresies, and pressure to organize the growing church gradually led bishops to "capture" and manage these spiritual gifts, until they were hardly seen or practiced among the laity.[19] By Augustine's time in the fifth century, this was the new normal.

Lack of space demands that we skip from the fall of Rome (AD 476) to the Reformation (1517), but (very) generally speaking, the intervening millennium was the high point of tradition. The institution of "the church" saw itself built on the foundation of the Bible but free to add doctrinal bricks atop it whenever "Christ's appointed successor" (the Pope, in Roman Catholicism; and, similarly though not identically, various Patriarchs in the Orthodox churches) so demanded. The power of the Spirit? You'd need a relic for that. The teaching of the Bible? There was a priest for that. Meeting to read and discuss God's word together, outside the structure of the institutional church? You'd be persecuted for that. Praying for revelation, insight, or healing? You'd likely be persecuted for that, too.

The Reformation can be viewed as the immune response of the body of Christ to the malignancy of tradition when it first supersedes and then chokes out biblical revelation. The cry of "Scripture alone" was the banner, and the Reformation's children deconstructed (and often destroyed) tradition. Scripture supplanted the supremacy of tradition, and the gospel was recovered, though not without cost.

---

19   James L. Ash, "The Decline of Ecstatic Prophecy in the Early Church," Theological Studies 36 (1976), 250.

Then, in the "new world" west of the Atlantic, the Spirit started to do a new thing. The Awakenings of the 18th and 19th centuries were the work of the Spirit combined with the preaching of God's word. Whole movements of missionaries were birthed at this time, and much of the Christian world that you and I know is a direct result of this period. With the dust of Reformation settling, it almost seemed like the band—Scripture, Spirit, and tradition— might be getting back together.

But the 20th century had a word to say about that. Modernity, industrialization, and the scientific revolution split the church once more. Many traditionalists went liberal, trading the gospel for acts of kindness—in other words, heretical. Many Scripturalists went fundamental, keeping the gospel but keeping everyone else out. Pentecostalism was growing but often became unmoored from the word, and was distrusted by the other tribes. And now, in the 21st century, we see Charismaticism continuing to shape the church in large parts of the world; a rise in the "gospel centrality" or "Young, Restless, and Reformed" movement in the US and elsewhere; and a renewed interest in church history and ancient Christian tradition.

So where does that leave us?

INTRODUCING TRILEMMIC DILIGENCE

Considering all we've learned so far, we can start to see what we lose when we lose one (or more) of word, Spirit, and tradition. Church history tells us that scriptural study and faithfulness makes and keeps the church biblical, and that's good. But without the Spirit and ignorant of tradition, we'll likely be unfruitful and unstable (think of all the church splits within Protestantism). On the other hand, the power and presence of the Spirit make the church fruitful, but without the Bible, fruit sours into error. And without tradition, we just repeat the mistakes of the past (Montanism is alive in well in parts of Pentecostalism). With discernment, tradition and history offer unique wisdom to us, showing us what other men and women of God taught, did, and even did wrong. As Tim Keller puts it, "Tradition gives a vote to the dead." But on the third hand (this is a trilemma—we can have three hands), subordinating God's living word to dead theologians corrodes biblical foundations. Formalizing the spiritual trades repetition for presence, leaving us fruitless, without the power to make any difference. (Empty traditional church buildings are everywhere, after all.)

So what might it look like to hold on to this Word-Spirit tension? The chart opposite shows what happens when we get it right (and wrong). The left side shows a low-tension state. Slide any category there and something important is sacrificed. The right side shows a high-tension state. There, the Bible is faithfully studied and proclaimed. The Spirit is powerfully present. And tradition connects us to the wisdom of the past. The result? Biblical, fruitful, stable faithfulness. But all this requires (and produces) a whole lot of diligence.

Read the Word

The Spirit wrote a book that tradition helps us to understand. So, read it. Every day. Serious saturation in the Scriptures means diligent, consistent marination in the stories, words, values, and the theology of our holy book of books. It means reading, confessing, and studying them, and, most importantly, obeying them. If you're new to the Bible, get a great church with trustworthy pastors to mentor and guide you. Ask them to guide you to their favorite dead theologians,

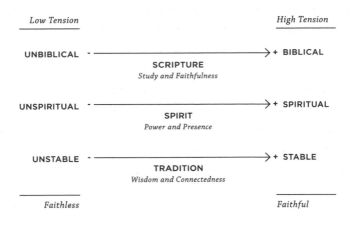

Low Tension		High Tension
UNBIBLICAL	-————————→	+ BIBLICAL
	SCRIPTURE	
	Study and Faithfulness	
UNSPIRITUAL	-————————→	+ SPIRITUAL
	SPIRIT	
	Power and Presence	
UNSTABLE	-————————→	+ STABLE
	TRADITION	
	Wisdom and Connectedness	
Faithless		*Faithful*

and let tradition seep into you. And, when you read, ask the Spirit to be present with you. Depending on your tribe, you'll have some repenting to do. But that's ok—we all do.

Respect Tradition

There's only one history of the church because to God there's only one church. We should learn some of our family history. Humility demands that we acknowledge the wisdom and courage of Bible-believing, Spirit-filled Christians who have gone before us, even at points where they were very different than us. Learn from them, especially the parts you don't like very much. All families have their bad moments— times when they wish they'd done things differently. The church is no different. It takes diligence to constantly ask ourselves, "What did Christians do when they faced this before?" Tradition highlights our current subconscious cultural assumptions and blindspots. Scripture says there's nothing new under the sun (Ecclesiastes 1 v 9), so we should view those believers who have gone before us as teachers and guides. The Spirit was with them, too, after all. It's cool today to point out the failures of past leaders—and there are times when it is right to—but criticism is easy. Deconstruction leaves everything, well, deconstructed. Maybe the most spiritual thing we could do in our present Word-Spirit tension is to open a history book with humble diligence. It may help us see how to hold the tension faithfully and fruitfully.

Be Filled with the Spirit

Following the word will require the Spirit. The Scriptures clearly, repeatedly, and strongly command us to seek an ongoing, abiding experience of God by seeking the ongoing, abiding experience of the Spirit.

- "Be continuously and repeatedly filled by the Spirit" (Ephesians 5 v 20, my translation)

- "Earnestly desire spiritual gifts..." (1 Corinthians 14 v 1). Here, the verb we translate as "earnestly desire" is very strong, sometimes even being translated as "to covet," or even "to be jealous for." That is how much we should be asking or and hoping for the Spirit to engift us, for the good of God's people.

- "Abide in me, and I in you" (John 15 v 4).

- "For this reason I remind you to fan into flame the gift of God" (2 Timothy 1 v 6). Here, Paul is encouraging his son in the Lord to grow in the gifts of God that were imparted to him through a Spirit-filling experience.

Love Unity

Jesus prayed for his church to be one (John 17 v 20-23). It's been hard for his people to be obedient to that prayer.

Disunity is always the other guy's fault, of course... but just for fun, look at yourself. Do you love unity? Does the word "Pentecostal" make you snicker or sneer? Do you think all Catholics are doomed for hell? Do you turn your nose up at guitars and lifted hands, preferring your pipe organ and written liturgy? Sin twists love for good things into disdain for what's different. But love "believes all things, hopes all things, and endures all things." It's patient and kind. How would you respond if a fellow Christian shared a prophetic vision? What would you say if someone in your cell group wanted to study Romans for a year? How might you react if a priest pulled up a chair and wanted to share his favorite stories of Christian history? We've got to go deeper than blogs, Facebook rants, and driveby comments on social media. God went out of his way to love us. We should consider doing the same.

OUR EMPIRES STRIKE BACK

Now, perhaps you're convinced that certain gifts have ceased (that is, you're a cessationist). Many Christians I respect hold this view, though I personally do not (and yes, I've studied the Scriptures, and I've read the greats of church history). I feel strongly convinced that the Bible teaches that all spiritual gifts still remain (the continuationist position). But this is not a book about that. This is, to my mind, so often the wrong question—a distracting canard from the enemy to keep God's people from the Word-Spirit-tradition reality. We stand rooted in tradition, under the authority of a text, filled with the Spirit who raised Christ from death. If I were the devil, I'd be really pleased by arguments over this gift or that and by mud-slinging from all sides that take the extreme ends of each and then assume that everyone in that camp is like that or (at best) on the slippery slope towards that. Not all slopes are slippery, and the top of a slope is called a peak, where all sides meet. The more we divide, the less Scripture we obey, the less of the Spirit we experience, and the less tradition we treasure. Fighting over tertiary questions keeps us from the first-place expectations that God has for his people: namely, to study the Scriptures, to be being filled with the Spirit, and to learn from tradition, not burn it down.

Ignoring tradition makes us fools.

Ignoring Scripture makes us sin.

Ignoring the Spirit makes us stagnate.

You can be a cessationist well, or poorly. You can be a continuationist biblically, or strangely. You can be a traditionalist and be biblically alive and fruit-bearing or you can be a traditionalist and be spiritually dead, disconnected from the Spirit and from the Scriptures. I'm not inviting you into my tribe *per se* (though you're welcome to join; the water is fine). I'm inviting us all into something far less comfortable and far more exciting—a word-Spirit-tradition tension that should upend all our tribes.

Resist the urge to remind yourself why you can't do this. That's your inner lawyer, prosecuting a case for the low-tension state of comfort—the happy familiarity of what we've always known. But what adventure awaits for the one who is diligent. I'll bet Mr. Zimmerman would befriend Pastor Jim. And I'll bet that if you take time to listen to, ask questions of, and give the benefit of the doubt to those who are in different tribes to you in this Word-Spirit-tradition tension, you'll be helped to think things through yourself, and to love those who are of the same Jesus-loving family but have different characteristics.

This is the great scheme of our one-in-three God: that by the Spirit-given word we would receive the word-promised Spirit. The Father, who planned redemption, sent the Son. The Son, who accomplished redemption, gave the gift of the Spirit. And the people of the Spirit have a long history in which the Spirit has, amid the human wrong turns and mistakes, worked through his people for their sanctification and for the good of the world. So, take the word seriously. Be filled with the Spirit ongoingly. Look to tradition regularly. What a church we would be.

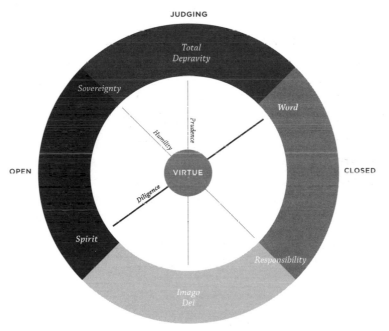

4. US *AND* THEM

"We must protect our borders."
Donald Trump, 2016

*"My dream is a hemispheric common market, with open
trade and open borders."*
Hillary Clinton, 2013

I was 24 when I had my first beer.

We were living in Edinburgh, Scotland, where my wife and I served a new church plant. My job: to disciple students and young adults. My success: dismal. I tried hard but was serially ignored. No matter what I did, I couldn't get these guys to talk with me. We'd banter about the weather and sports, of course. But when it came to matters of God and the gospel, they'd ghost.

Expressing this frustration at church one Sunday, my peers chuckled.

"What's so funny?" I said, annoyed.

"Men here don't open up except in one place—the pub."

They knew this would bother me, thus the levity. I'd rebuffed their invitation to the pub a time or two. A teetotaler, I didn't just not drink alcohol; I hated it. And not without reason: everyone in my family, going back generations, has had an addiction problem of one kind or another. My childhood gave me a front-row seat to view the destructive power of drinking and drug abuse. In adulthood I wanted nothing to do with any of it.

If you'd asked me, I'd have said that, while I abstained from drinking, other Christians were free to drink alcohol, according to their consciences (as in 1 Corinthians 10 v 23-32). I'd probably have smiled, too. But that smile on my face would have masked the judgment in my heart. There were two kinds of Christians to me: the ones who avoided alcohol, and the ones who were wrong. How could I enter a pub to make disciples? To me, that was enemy territory.

So you can imagine my annoyance at that suggestion.

I carried on in my ways, but I didn't make much headway. Eventually, I re-examined my opposition. I was, after all, a missionary. Hundreds of people were praying for me, and many were also financially supporting me. They were rooting for me to be fruitful. So I relented a bit. If it meant getting a gospel opportunity, I'd nurse a soft drink in this den of iniquity.

Before long, an opportunity came. Two young men attended an outreach event, and I followed up with them. As expected, they invited me to join them at their local pub, and I agreed. I showed up and ordered a soda, and the conversation got started, me with cola and them with their pints. I began to try to engage them with the message of Jesus, but they seemed more curious about my selection of beverage than my Savior's message. The night ended, the conversation rarely having moved beyond my beerlessness.

I departed, even more frustrated. That was the last meeting I had with those young men.

Frustrated, I came back to my friends the next Sunday. "All right," I said. "Looks like one of you is going to have to teach me something about beer."

ARBITRARY BOUNDARIES

Silly as it seems, this experience illustrates a small border skirmish between "us" and "them." Now, there are good reasons not to drink. Obviously, you needn't drink to be a fruitful evangelist, nor must you avoid alcohol to be a faithful disciple. But looking back, for me this whole episode wasn't about avoiding beer but enforcing a border. I had more fear about what laid beyond it than faith in God to sustain me through it. My side was the "right" side. On the other side lay immorality and a slippery slope down into the sins of my fathers. Eventually the Spirit and the Scriptures revealed my heart, and I was able to move past a strongly-held preference to embrace greater obedience.

Ironically, I've now lost count of the fruitful evangelistic and deep discipleship conversations I've had over drinks that I once disdained. The men I've introduced to Jesus are probably glad that God won that argument. But I still had to navigate a tension between "us" Christians and "them" worldly folks (or "us" mature Christians and "them" misguided believers) in order to bear spiritual fruit. I still do. We all do—because we all enforce borders, even if they fall in different places for you than for me.

It's important to recognize that we usually build walls for good reasons. From people who hurt us to a past that still haunts us, it's natural and often wise to exclude the things that have truly harmed us. But where the Scriptures relegate matters to conscience (like drinking, for example) we mustn't elevate them to universal law obedience. And I did. I catastrophized a matter of conscience into a border war—a silly side fight that kept me the good one. Your border probably isn't over beers, but perhaps it's Brexit. Maybe it's parenting, or politics. "It's so obvious," you say, "that a Christian would vote *this* way." Or "Godly people can't go to *those* places"—wherever "those" places happen to be. And let's not even discuss *those* people.

The inclusivist/exclusivist debate describes how those inside the borders of the group, nation, or church ask, "How far should we go in including/excluding outsiders?" But those outside the boundaries ask, "Why won't they let me in?" This debate rages in our politics, on our campuses, in our nations, and through our church tribal affiliations. This compels some of us to patrol the borders of our particular group, enforcing moral codes, special words, and purity tests—the barbarians are never far from the gates, we insist, and we need to stand on the ramparts keeping watch. For others this debate demands that all the walls fall, so that everyone is accepted, shouting, "All are welcome!" (Except, of course, those who don't welcome all people in the way we'd like.) The excluders demand walls while the includers want doors. On one side, boundaries. On the other side, bridges.

This tension confuses us. We're Christians—we want to be welcoming. Yet, we're Christians—there are limits. Where do we land? Follow some Christians and you'll get a stream of proof-texts on the importance of purity, demanding that we diligently hold the line against the depravity of the culture. Follow others and you'll get a different scriptural selection about welcoming the migrant, the sojourner, and the outsider, demanding that we demolish the walls for the sake of the world.

So what side does the Bible land on?

Well, by now, you must know that that's a trick question...

THE BIBLE AND ITS BORDERS

On one reading, the Bible is a very exclusivist story. God makes humans and sets them in a garden sanctuary with clear boundaries. *Do this,* he says: "Be fruitful, multiply, and subdue the earth" (Genesis 1 v 28). *Don't do this*: "Don't eat of the tree of knowledge" (2 v 17). Our ancestors failed, and they were excluded from God's presence (3 v 24), God guarding the border back to Eden with a terrifying angel wielding a flaming sword. When their son Cain killed their other child Abel, he was excluded from God's family (4 v 14). Later, God commanded his national family, Israel, to not mix with the godless tribes around them. Transgressing this boundary led them to suffer invasion and eventual exile (2 Kings 17). Later again, Jesus' work brought God's people back across the border, making them citizens of heaven (Ephesians 2 v 19). But still, in the end, God will separate the *us* who love Jesus from the *them* who don't, welcoming his children to his heavenly banquet, and excluding those who reject him by shutting them out in the darkness (Luke 13 v 22-29).

Is all that true? Yes. Is it the whole truth? No.

On a different reading, the Bible is a yearningly inclusive story. Setting humans in the garden sanctuary, God invites them to join in his creational project of border expansion (Genesis 1 v 28). Even when they break his heart and his law (Genesis 3), he promises to defeat their enemy (v 15) so that he might welcome them back into his presence once again. He pleads with Cain to remain in faith (4 v 7) and includes the pagan Abram in his project to bless those of every nation (Genesis 12). Israel is created to bless the world (18 v 18) as a light to the nations (Isaiah 42 v 6; 49 v 6). Even in failure and exile, prophets foretold a global redemption. Jesus came to end this spiritual exile and make good on those prophetic promises, inviting those from far and wide to come into his kingdom, no matter what they had done. In the end, God will defeat evil and open the doors of the eternal city to all who trust in the Son (Revelation 21 v 25).

Is that also true? Absolutely. Is it the whole truth? Again, no.

The truth is that Bible says that there's a big border between the "us" of God's people and the "them" of the world, and crossing it means sinful complicity with God's enemies. Yet it demands that the "us" of God's people go to "them" in the world and bring our God and his gospel with us, working hard to include them among us. The truth is that the Bible is both radically inclusive and uncompromisingly exclusive. Us-and-them matters fundamentally, and it matters not at all.

It's quite a tension.

ELECT EXILES

Are we to exclude sinners and maintain purity in the church, or are we to welcome outsiders, and seek those beyond the borders of our churches to include in the people of God?

Well, yes, as a matter of fact.

I'm not being snarky—just scriptural. Since its explosive origin at Pentecost, the church has tried to traverse this tension. The leap from a small Jewish sect to an international, multiethnic movement led to the first debate among the apostolic fathers (Acts 15). How would they hold together a uniquely Jewish movement that was adding lots of non-Jews? Would they exclude the non-Jews? Should they demand that they *become* Jews? Or was the answer to include non-Jews by removing the boundary lines that formerly kept Jew and non-Jews apart?

After intense debate, prayer, and study, the Spirit led them to say this to the multitudes who were putting their hope and faith in this Jewish Messiah: "We should not trouble those of the Gentiles who turn to God, but should write to them to abstain from the things polluted by idols, and from sexual immorality, and from what has been strangled, and from blood" (Acts 15 v 19–20). They included them... and they included moral boundaries. Inclusion and exclusion.

Later, speaking into the same growing Jesus movement, Peter gave Christians the name "elect exiles," (1 Peter 1 v 1). This was a people chosen to be separate from the world, yet those sent by God to be messengers in it.

In one sense, there is no more inclusive word in the Bible than the word "elect." If salvation is all of God (and it is), then no one is beyond the capability of the gospel to save. No one has a right to be included; but no one cannot be included. And the elect are brought right into the family of God—not as servants so much as friends. God includes us in the closest possible relationship with him, so that we—whoever we are, whatever we've done, wherever we're from—by faith call him "Abba": *dad*.

Yet here the word "elect" sits beside the radically exclusive word "exiles." Peter assigned it to God's new Israel, to remind them that they were not the same as the world, could never live as though there was no difference between them and everyone else, and would never fit in here. That's the church: the radically included, intentionally excluded.

Not only that, but the word "exile" haunted Jewish memory, reminding them of God's punishment for idolatry and disobedience. It is a word that speaks of God's uncompromising determination to exclude what is unholy from his presence. His people live as missionary exiles, warning of the threat of eternal exile even as we announce the end of exile for *all* human sinfulness through the work of Jesus. God is holy, yet in Jesus he was wholly committed to walking through the muddy wreckage of sin to make the world holy, too. Elected for exile on Golgotha's hill, Jesus rose, ending exile for God's elect people.

"US-ING" VS. "THEM-ING"

When I was an undergrad, my religion professor—a large, German man with a Bond-villain accent—opened his first class declaring, "Here, you'll learn to see the world larger, and become a more inclusive practitioner of your own faith." Inclusion was the goal and exclusion the enemy. In lecture after lecture he taught how exclusivism saw its followers bomb abortion clinics, fly planes into buildings, and deny minorities human rights. He insisted that these outcomes were the direct result of religions that built walls separating insiders from outsiders. But now, he insisted, we (by which I think he meant people who thought like him) knew better, and religion had to catch up with the times. Popular atheistic writing uses this argument too. Religion, atheists say, makes people afraid of others, so that they hatefully exclude them and foment

violence toward them.[20] Today, exclusion—not unbelief—
is the unforgivable sin. The only thing that can and must
be excluded is exclusion itself (along with all those mean
excluders).

We should be suspicious of any idea that has as its
conclusion a logical contradiction. Excluding excluders
doesn't sound very inclusive, after all. But it gets worse.
To say, "The belief that my faith is true and yours false
(exclusivism) is wrong and should be abandoned (for
inclusivism, presumably)," is simply to make a new
exclusive claim: "We must exclude the exclusivists."
This statement violates the very principle it propounds.
Moving the boundaries of exclusion won't make you more
inclusive, only innovatively exclusive. The boundaries are
still there; they just exclude a new group. Now they exclude
the exclusivists.

Offenses against the law of non-contradiction aside,
though, a good point is being made here—and if you nodded
along enthusiastically to my take-down of the position in
the previous paragraph, slow your nodding and strap in.
Exclusivists have done terrible things. Crusades, jihads,
and sectarian violence mark the history of world religions
like craters on a battlefield. And, of course, there are plenty
of secular exclusive creeds that have scarred history and
the present.

This contest between inclusion and exclusion is presently
confounding Western democracies. Half of us want to build
walls and break away from the others, while the other half
want to obliterate borders and welcome all. Feeding on

---

20 This is the view of books such as Christopher Hitchens, *God is Not
    Great* (Twelve, 2009) and Sam Harris, *The End of Faith* (W.W. Norton,
    2005).

fear that foments to hate, exclusion can tend to tribalism and racism. Pathologizing empathy, inclusion can lead to authoritarianism and pride. The excluder demands a certain kind stay out. The includer demands everyone be welcomed in, and every opinion be welcomed too (except for those pesky opinions that includers don't like).

Politics therefore provides sharp contrasts between exclusion and embrace, and the anxiety and anger is palpable. The utopia that prosperity and connectivity promised to give us not only hasn't materialized, but instead a lurching hell of loneliness and anxiety has grown. Pretty much no one—from politicians to philosophers—has any idea of how to handle this well. Our leaders offer new ways to include or exclude, but trying again what's already failed is unlikely to suddenly succeed. Apart from God's presence, the problem is unsolvable and the tension unmanageable.

Frequently, the church fares no better. Christians are neither sure where and how to build appropriate walls nor where and how to install much-needed doors. Sadly, some saints specialize in debates that define the rightness of us and the wrongness of "them"—be they the "them" of the world or the "them" of a different tribe within the church. We can make "thems" over anything—drinking alcohol, the use of spiritual gifts, the number of angels we think can fit on a pinhead, or the type of chairs that we decide redeemed rears ought to occupy. (I exaggerate, but not much.)

This tendency—the impulse to hunker down, build walls, and hurl invective—is precisely what we should avoid when it comes to biblical tensions.

So, how do we move forward?

INCLUSIVE EXCLUSIVISM, EXCLUSIVE INCLUSIVISM

Put (fairly) simply, Scripture leads us to inclusive exclusivism and exclusive inclusivism. And grasping this will see us grow in kindness.

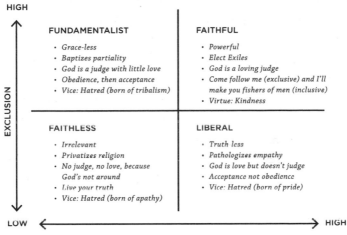

HIGH

FUNDAMENTALIST
- Grace-less
- Baptizes partiality
- God is a judge with little love
- Obedience, then acceptance
- Vice: Hatred (born of tribalism)

FAITHFUL
- Powerful
- Elect Exiles
- God is a loving judge
- Come follow me (exclusive) and I'll make you fishers of men (inclusive)
- Virtue: Kindness

EXCLUSION

FAITHLESS
- Irrelevant
- Privatizes religion
- No judge, no love, because God's not around
- Live your truth
- Vice: Hatred (born of apathy)

LIBERAL
- Truth less
- Pathologizes empathy
- God is love but doesn't judge
- Acceptance not obedience
- Vice: Hatred (born of pride)

LOW   HIGH

INCLUSION

In the chart above are four quadrants. Along the X-axis, inclusion charts from low to high, and along the Y-axis exclusion is in similar form. Quadrant 1 (low inclusion and low exclusion) represents faithlessness. Caring neither for exclusive truth nor inclusive grace, this is the tribe of privatized religious sentiment: God is acknowledged, but in a distant, managerial way, rendering him (and this position) irrelevant. In this position people are happy for others to believe what they please, which initially seems tolerant. But this is an apathetic tolerance. Caring not at all for anyone else, it breeds apathy—that careless self-interest, which, at bottom, is hate.

Quadrant 2 (high inclusion, low exclusion) is the home of liberals. Led by their empathy and a desire not to exclude, they end up with a God who is too agreeable to ever *dis*agree with any of us. "God is love," they repeat, forgetting that God's love is the bloody cross of his Son to bring satisfaction for sin (1 John 4 v 10). Such cancerous empathy feels badly for anyone on the other side of the fence of truth. "God wouldn't exclude anyone," they argue—and he wouldn't, *if* they come in repentance and faith. But the problem is that this position ends up refusing to exclude anyone who refuses to repent. And it leads to the strange pride of believing you're the most accepting person in the room, and, eventually, to an intolerant disdain of anyone who doesn't accept people like you do. In its final stages, this cancerous confusion metastasizes in an inability to call evil "evil," insisting that doing so is the only evil there is.

Quadrant 3 represents the fundamentalists. These come with church clothes and make their life's work to keep those clothes "unstained from the world." Armed with the truth, their arsenal lacks grace, making God a loveless, cosmic judge who cares more about law-keeping than relationship. At best, this kind of exclusivist keeps at arm's length Christians who don't sign up to their every position, sneers at brothers who disagree, and, preaching to the choir, tears down those who ask questions or do things differently. At worst, this position trends toward a racist, xenophobic kind of hate. Insisting it has the truth on its side, it resents those on the other side, and (just like the others) becomes like the false god it worships—a loveless judge.

The final quadrant is for elect exiles. The faithful are included excluders, inviting everyone to experience acceptance through the Son and warning that without him there is no hope for salvation. They're also excluded includers—sent to a world that, despite the inclusive invitation, will fundamentally reject him, and them. God's inclusive invitation to every tribe, tongue, people, and nation demands of us a decision. That word itself is exclusive—coming from two Latin roots meaning "to cut apart." There's no version of biblical Christianity that simply includes anyone any more than there's a version that excludes everyone.

Holding this elect-exile, inclusion-exclusion tension takes work. How do we avoid the three hates of tribalistic exclusion, of smug, authoritarian inclusion, and of the apathetic disregard of personal religion? Or—more provocatively—how do we see that we've landed there, and move towards faithful tension?

Truth and Grace Bring Change

Jesus showed up with grace and truth (John 1 v 17). We have to show up that way too. Graceless, "drive-by shootings" of Scripture in comments sections or social media neither honor God nor bear fruit. Truth-free "tolerance" doesn't save. Only the exclusive truth of God's inclusive grace in the gospel transforms. It is kind to warn and it is kind to woo. Ask yourself: would a Christian who knows me fairly well, and who does not hold all my positions, say that I'm committed both to truth and to grace? To right doctrine and deep devotion? What about a non-believing neighbor or colleague?

Beware Empathy, Pursue Compassion

Decades of Disney, pop psychology, and cultural Christianity have exalted empathy masquerading as virtue. We think with our hearts. Empathy, a word added to the English language in 1909, has gone from academic obscurity to cultural supremacy.[21] To "feel with" others is important for compassion, of course; but it is totally irrelevant for knowing what's true. Truth-tempered empathy can be a powerful remedy. But truthless empathy breeds selective Christianity—one that picks sides by feelings instead of faith. Beware your empathetic heart. It can tell great lies (Jeremiah 17 v 9). Equally, beware your uncompassionate heart. Ignoring others, intentionally misrepresenting their views, and castigating one for whom Christ died is loveless. Love listens, thinks, learns, and still says when necessary, "But here is the truth, no matter how we feel."

Partiality Is Always a Problem

We all have a bent. Our ethnicity, social mobility, nationality, and dozens of other factors form our boundaries—our preferences, moral sentiments, and political persuasions, to name a few. We imagine we arrive at those conclusions through research and reason, but we don't.[22] Our age has blinded us to our partiality—the biblical, umbrella term for all the -isms (racism, classism, sexism, agism, and so on) and phobias (homophobia, xenophobia, and so on). This problem stands before and behind all the others, and it is immovably imbedded in us unless and until gospel truth and grace change us. Kindness means seeing my prejudices and presuppositions, having sympathy for others with theirs, and being willing to see

---

21 Susan Lanzoni, "A Short History of Empathy," in The Atlantic (October 15, 2015) (theatlantic.com/health/archive/2015/10/a-short-history-of-empathy/409912, accessed 4.20.20).

22 In his book *The Righteous Mind* (Pantheon, 2012), Jonathan Haidt demonstrates the psychological research which undermines the idea that our preferences and moral sentiments are formed by our conscious, thinking selves. He shows that most of these formations are pre-cognitive and non-rational.

where my boundary may be based more on my upbringing or preference than on Scripture.

SOME WALLS MUST STAND, SOME MUST FALL

The border of belief in the gospel must stand. Borders differentiate one country from another, and the gospel differentiates the people of God from the people of this world. Scriptural authority is likewise an irrevocable boundary—and therefore so are the sexual, financial, and personal moralities that it sets forth. Words are walls—borders of belief—defining the faith "once for all delivered" (Jude v 3). For Jesus did "not come to bring peace, but a sword ... to set a man against his father, and a daughter against her mother, and a daughter-in-law against her mother-in-law" (Matthew 10 v 34-35). For every Christian in every age and every place there will be those who demand that we move the fences of our faith to more nicely conform to the contours of the culture. And when they do, we must offer a loving but immovable "no."

The "no" of the martyrs brought Rome to its knees. The "no" of Reformers fueled gospel faith. The "no" of liberators caused slavery to cease. We are an "us-and-them" people, and tearing down the fences of our faith because the world prefers or demands it is foolishness and faithlessness (Proverbs 22 v 28).

But while some walls must stand, others must fall.

Dividing ourselves along partiality's fault lines (of preference, language, aesthetics, race, class, and so on) is disobedience. Being a church that excludes those not like us or elevates matters of conscience to a boundary completely undermines the whole point of the church's mission in this world. Jesus' exclusive announcement above continues with a warning that there are immovable boundaries, but it finishes with an inclusive twist:

> *"Whoever loves father or mother more than me is not worthy of me, and whoever loves son or daughter more than me is not worthy of me. And whoever does not take his cross and follow me is not worthy of me. Whoever finds his life will lose it, and whoever loses his life for my sake will find it." (Matthew 10 v 36-39)*

Don't miss the challenge: if we love our preferences more than we love Jesus, we exclude ourselves from Jesus. Dying to partiality is profoundly difficult—a daily cross—but it is demanded by our Savior.

Here is the tension: faithfulness to exclusive gospel truth means embodying inclusive gospel grace. It means removing every barrier other than the gospel. Faithfulness is not about sitting idly behind the border of our political preference, worship style, favorite doctrines, cultural norms, and postal codes, and merely praying for "those people." "Those people" are precisely who Jesus is talking about. Going to them may mean we've got to demolish a large section of wall and build a long bridge with a big door.

We have a long history of getting this wrong. The multiethnic mission of the early church utterly scandalized the world around them. Several of the apostles once thought that church should only be for ethnic Jews. The Pope once commanded the armies of Europe to obliterate Muslims. Evangelical pastors refused a missionary named William Carey a commission to evangelize "heathen" India. Some American Christians supported (and took part in) the racist exclusion of black men and women. By God's grace, these walls fell down. So must the walls hiding in our hearts.

Christian love strives to include as many as will trust in King Jesus. Such love will cost you your preference, your comfort, and the norms of your culture—it cost Christ his, too. But here's the promise: embracing this tension forms in us the kindness of Jesus.

MEET JESUS, THE EXCLUDED EXCLUDING INCLUDER

Heaven has high walls. Behind them, God's glorious presence is on full display. Beyond them, the very tragedy of humanity is in full view. Christ moved beyond the walls of his home to come scandalously close. Divine-human Jesus included us *through* his exclusion, when he died outside the city walls. His kingdom includes the worst sinners from the whole world. The invitation is completely inclusive and totally exclusive. There's only one Savior, yet anyone may come to him to be saved.

We are *not* the world, and we're not to be like the world. We are called to go into the world, and from it to make disciples. We *are* the church. We're not to pretend that doctrines and practices we differ over do not matter. We are called to teach the whole counsel of God, not a watered-down gospel. Yet at the same time we are not to other-ize fellow gospel-believers, showing them how wrong they are and how right we are. Yet this is exactly what we've done—denominations, worship styles, pet doctrines, and preferred practices have been the devil's playthings. Therefore, we need the Spirit's help. We must hold this tension. And, as the Spirit helps us, he'll give us fruit too—the virtue of kindness. Kindness toward the world and kindness toward the church. Imagine that—Christians, anxiety-free, embracing the sinner, explaining the truth, and refusing to cower.

For me, this meant kindly cross-bearing over a preference and having a beer with some students. What about you? Maybe less drinking, and more differentiating holiness—a less proud, more profound obedience. It could require reimagining your church services, being willing to move away from your preferences. It probably requires rethinking your behavior on social media. It definitely demands loving those people, despite what they've said or done—praying for, or even with, those with whom you disagree. The truth in the tension between exclusion and embrace goes beyond doctrinal accuracy. It enables a life lived more virtuously—a kindness that is formed in the furnace of the fight to obey God's word while inviting the world. The only question is, will you step into that furnace so he can form kindness in you?

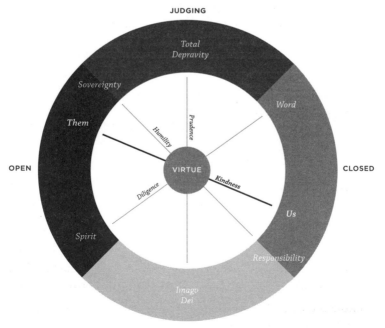

5. VICTORY *AND* SUFFERING

"The magic to attain victory is simple... just believe."
Omoakhuana Anthonia

"Life is suffering, and suffering can make you resentful, murderous, and then genocidal, if you take it far enough. So you need an antidote to suffering."
Jordan Peterson

"We got the victory! We got the victory!!"
The music was loud, the people were jumping, and the energy in the room was contagious. As I sang these unfamiliar lyrics, I was unknowingly beginning a new stage in my faith journey. I say "unknowingly" because at the time I would have simply said that I'd started going to a new church while in university—a church rather different than the more mild ones from which I came. Looking back, this new church experience marked the beginning of my sojourn among a new tribe of Christians—Christians who expected that God would give them, in the moment of their trials, complete victory.

The word "victory" was used a lot. The message of resurrection victory was preached. The power of Christ's victory was applied—to the struggle against sin, the world, and the devil. A culture of victorious living flourished there, and it was a heady time for me—one which God used to teach me much about faith and how to trust him for things that had previously seemed impossible to me.

While my memory of these times is good, I also remember bumping into some strange outworkings of this teaching from time to time.

"Disease is a choice," she said.

"What? What do you mean?" I asked.

"Look, if Jesus defeated disease at the cross, and if there is no disease in God's kingdom, then the only reason you and I and any other Christian suffer from disease is because, on some level, we choose to. We can learn to walk in victory over disease."

That awkward conversation—and others like it—highlights the troubled border between the victory we were all hoping to "walk in" and the suffering that life entails. Among these "victorious" Christians, I was busy making up for a rather large "vitamin deficiency" in my own understanding of the Christian life. But as I consumed all this teaching about faith and victory, I found that alongside me some (not all) fellow church members had other vitamins in short supply. Indeed, the pill of suffering is hard to swallow.

That church experience took place years ago. And, yes, I still believe that there is more victory waiting for most of us than we currently have faith to receive. But as I write these words, my family and I are walking through what is the most difficult trial of our lives. The last year has been pockmarked with suffering—there are craters on the landscape of an otherwise happy scrapbook of memories for a young pastor-scholar and his family. The nature of the struggle is such that putting its details in print would be inappropriate, but suffice it to say that a close member of our family is passing through a season of deep suffering, and we're all walking through it too. It has been over a year of painful experiences, countless tears, emotional rollercoasters, and sleepless nights—the kind of year that makes some shake their fists at the heavens, accusing God of callous malevolence.

Yet, I have not done so. And I will not do so.

I am living in the tension between victory and suffering. But that's not unique to me. As we'll see, we will all dwell in this tension at some time, if we have not already. The question for the apprentice of Jesus is neither how to avoid suffering nor how to have victory. The right question is how can we navigate this tension well enough to live in it like Jesus.

GOD GIVES US VICTORY

I don't know you, but my educated guess is that you're either the kind of person who generally expects things to go well or the kind of person who doesn't. If you're the former, you'll be thrilled to know that the Bible gives us great reasons to expect great things from our great God. If you're the latter, you'll view this section with suspicion. So this is a moment to admit who you are to yourself and embrace the challenge of hearing Scriptures that, if you trust the God who inspired them, communicate to you promises that are actually yours. As we'll see, even the optimists among us haven't hoped for a future this bright.

The Bible begins as a victory story. God makes the world, and after six days of bringing chaos into order, order into life, and life into image-bearing humanity, God rests. And not because he is exhausted from work. No, he rests like a warrior who has won a battle, like an artist who has finally tamed raw marble into sculpture, like a composer who has structured sounds into a symphony.

The story of the Bible is a victory story.

The Old Testament tells us about a series of unlikely victories, wrought by the God who wrought the first one. Noah was led to victory over judgment's flood. Abraham was led in victory over his enemies, his strange family, and his infertile body. Moses led the people of Israel in victory over their Egyptian captors, God defeating his enemies and rescuing Israel's family. Space doesn't permit me to tell the stories of Gideon, Samson, and David—all flawed men who all experienced unimaginable victories in life and in battle. And the Old Testament doesn't just give victory stories—it gives victory promises. Among them all, I find these, given to Moses and Israel after the exodus, most striking:

> *"And if you faithfully obey the voice of the Lord your God, being careful to do all his commandments that I command you today, the Lord your God will set you high above all the nations of the earth. And all these blessings shall come upon you and overtake you, if you obey the voice of the Lord your God. Blessed shall you be in the city, and blessed shall you be in the field. Blessed shall be the fruit of your womb and the fruit of your ground and the fruit of your cattle, the increase of your herds and the young of your flock. Blessed shall be your basket and your kneading*

*bowl. Blessed shall you be when you come in, and blessed
shall you be when you go out.*

*"The LORD will cause your enemies who rise against you to
be defeated before you. They shall come out against you
one way and flee before you seven ways. The LORD will
command the blessing on you in your barns and in all that
you undertake. And he will bless you in the land that the
LORD your God is giving you. The LORD will establish you
as a people holy to himself, as he has sworn to you, if you
keep the commandments of the LORD your God and walk
in his ways. And all the peoples of the earth shall see that
you are called by the name of the LORD, and they shall
be afraid of you. And the LORD will make you abound in
prosperity, in the fruit of your womb and in the fruit of
your livestock and in the fruit of your ground, within the
land that the LORD swore to your fathers to give you. The
LORD will open to you his good treasury, the heavens, to
give the rain to your land in its season and to bless all the
work of your hands. And you shall lend to many nations,
but you shall not borrow. And the LORD will make you the
head and not the tail, and you shall only go up and not
down." (Deuteronomy 28 v 1-13)*

Look at those promises. Don't theologize them yet. Just
look at them, slowly. Before you start recounting all the
historical reasons why Israel never walked in them, just
read them. "Blessings" that "overtake you..." "The LORD
will command the blessing on you..." Do you hear the
intentions of your Father? Can you suspend disbelief long
enough to see his desires for his people?

If you're like me, you're so jaded that it's hard to read words
like this. So when we come to a book like Proverbs, filled with

wisdom for success and godly living—like "Whoever walks in integrity walks securely" (10 v 9) or "A generous person will prosper" (11 v 25)—it takes less than a second for us to (mis)use the next book, Ecclesiastes, to undercut and scoff about these things. But the Bible promises keep coming. Psalms sing of God's power, promises, and victory. The prophets give hope for Israel's coming victories, and even God's cosmic victory (see Isaiah 47 – 56; Jeremiah 31; Daniel 7; Ezekiel 11 v 14-25). Then all that God promises about future victories comes charging into the present in the presence of Jesus.

His life was victorious over all sin. His death defeated death. His resurrection put hell, demons, and the false king of this world to shame. And his ascension began the final, unlooked-for twist in God's ultimate cosmic victory over evil. The powerful presence of the same Spirit that raised Jesus is raising up the church, until the day of Christ's return. Just as God rested after the first creation, we will rest in Christ's new creation and experience a final victory that no present pain can take away (1 Peter 1 v 4), and with which no present joy can compare (Philippians 1 v 23; Psalm 84 v 10). So real is our future victory with Christ that Paul said we are already seated in victory with him (Ephesians 2 v 6), and Jesus himself taught us to longingly expect it in every prayer that echoes his words, "your kingdom come," even as he promises, "I have overcome [literally "won a victory over"] the world," (John 16 v 33). His is a kingdom of victory, and his kingdom is ours.

GOD GIVES US SUFFERING

If all you had was the previous section, and all you read were the previous Scriptures, then you would be an adherent of that most deplorable of modern heresies, the "prosperity gospel." But we must be clear about why such a heresy is deplorable. It is not that this fake gospel—the false good news that God always, only, ever wants to bless you, heal you, and enrich you by faith—is not biblical. It's that it's not biblical *enough*. Because God doesn't *only* promise victory. He promises a good deal of suffering too.

It is true that the Bible begins as a victory story. But it almost immediately turns tragic, as the chaos that God just ordered comes roaring back through the rebellion of the first humans (Genesis 3). The two chapters of creation are followed by three chapters of horrific evil, unleashed into the good world God made. This all culminates in the time of Noah, when judgment waters slowly deprive men and women mired in sin of the breath of life.

The story of the Bible, and of the lives of our spiritual forefathers, is one of suffering.

Abraham blinks at God's promises, sleeps with Hagar, and becomes the father of the very people who would harass Isaac's family forever. Moses leads Israel out of Egypt, but on the way to victory in the promised land they all sin, they all suffer, and they are all (save for Joshua and Caleb) denied entry. Space doesn't permit me to recount the tragedies of Gideon (who became an idolater), Samson (a reckless murderer), and David (an adulterer whose own family betrayed him, destroying him emotionally). And while I find the promises of Deuteronomy 28 most wonderful, I cannot tell you to meditate on them without also telling you that the section that follows them is filled with terrible curses for sin, and is four times longer.

If you're like me, you're so jaded that it's pretty easy to see this. The sarcastic tone of Ecclesiastes sounds about right, and the sobbing poetry of Lamentations is spot on. While Psalms has a lot of victory songs, there are many tracks on that album that are written in a minor key. The same prophets who promised a victorious future penned those words among paragraphs of pain. They excoriated Israel for their disobedience, warning of sufferings still to come.

But the worst suffering of all wasn't given by God to us but received by God the Son. His betrayal was a tragedy. His trial was a mockery. His torturous beating was more than most of us could have borne. And his death was a slow, throbbing acquiescence to the suffering that he neither caused nor deserved. When he breathed his last, the sky turned the color of bruised flesh as the God of the universe was murdered on a splintered beam overlooking the city dump.

Jesus said, "A servant is not greater than his master. If they persecuted me, they will persecute you also" (John 15 v 20). Peter, Paul, James, and John all penned letters warning their readers to avoid sin and to persevere despite the pain. The first three of those men died a martyr's death, bearing witness to the victory of King Jesus; the fourth was exiled to an island, far from fellow Christians. The church is called to followed their example. Centuries later, the church father Tertullian wrote, *"Semen est sanguis Christianorum"*—"The blood of martyrs is the seed of the church." Jesus himself promised, "In this life you will have tribulation" (John 16 v 33). No exceptions, no exemptions. Simply suffering as expectation. Whether we suffer because of bad choices, mistreatment, natural disaster, or mysterious circumstance, that future-tense promise for Jesus is a present-tense reality for us.

HOW CAN THESE THINGS GO TOGETHER?

If all you had was the previous section you would be in no danger of the huckster scams of the prosperity gospel; you'd experience different liabilities. At risk of becoming a cynic or an ascetic, you could embrace either the belief that God is not good and holy or the belief that pain and suffering are good and holy. So, holding on to all of Deuteronomy 28 is not optional—it's essential. We mustn't just say, "Well, it feels like suffering and victory can't go together" and stop there. We must carry on by saying, "But Scripture clearly teaches that they do go together—so, how?"

Since I've quoted twice from the same verse in John, let's see the whole thing together. John 16 v 33 says, "I have said these things to you, that in me you may have peace. In the world you will have tribulation. But take heart; I have overcome the world." The Greek words behind the English words "tribulation" and "overcome" are the same words that get translated elsewhere as (yup, you guessed it) "suffering" and "victory" respectively. So here's King Jesus, our great deliverer, teacher, Master, and Savior, saying, *I promise you two things: you're going to suffer in this world, and I have won a victory over this world.* Should it be such a wonder, then, that the people of God should expect to walk as he walked?

Consider the top-charting song of all time: Psalm 23.

"The LORD is my shepherd; I shall not want.
He makes me lie down in green pastures.
He leads me beside still waters.
He restores my soul.
He leads me in paths of righteousness
for his name's sake." (v 1-3)

Those parts we like. Sounds like victory, doesn't it? But wait—he goes on:

> *"Even though I walk through the valley of the shadow of*
> *death,*
> *I will fear no evil,*
> *for you are with me;*
> *your rod and your staff,*
> *they comfort me.*
> *You prepare a table before me*
> *in the presence of my enemies." (v 4-5)*

Wait, what happened to the pretty water and green pastures? Why did we leave? The composer moves beyond beautiful vistas because that's not what he's selling us. He's selling us a path of the righteous—a path rooted in God's shepherding goodness. We lack nothing with him, but if we're going to follow Jesus as our Lord, then we'll most certainly walk through shadowy valleys and deathly deserts. We'll have enemies, and life will get hard. But that doesn't mean he's not still a good shepherd, leading us to victory; it just means we're still on the road of righteousness. And even there, he will prepare a table for us. We can dine with our Shepherd while in the valley of suffering, with enemies all around. And when we learn to do that, what is the promise?

> *"You anoint my head with oil;*
> *my cup overflows.*
> *Surely goodness and mercy shall follow me*
> *all the days of my life,*
> *and I shall dwell in the house of the* LORD
> *forever." (v 6)*

Goodness and mercy chase us down, even in the valley. And if we keep hold of the tension, and we keep going, we will dwell in God's space forever. That's a victory that, in some strange way, is made all the better for the suffering. These aren't contradictions; they are complementary truths that, if we will hear their wisdom, shape us to be more like Jesus as we navigate life's cool streams, dark valleys, and hairpin turns.

HOLD THE TENSION, HONE THE VIRTUE

So, crosses give way to resurrections. Judgment acquiesces to Jesus' return. The Jesus story imbues those who trust in it with more than enough explanatory power for faith's victory and life's suffering.

That's what shaped Paul's words when he encouraged another group of victorious sufferers by telling them that "this light, momentary affliction is producing for us a weight of glory beyond all compare" (2 Corinthians 4 v 17). Hear that—the affliction is, in God's hands, producing glory, not diminishing it.

Much is at stake if we let go of the truth taught in the tension of victory and suffering. As I've said, the victory-only crew looks tempting. Prosperity, nice homes, beautiful bodies, and full bank accounts are the promised reward for those who learn to use their faith to make a way! But this theology turns out to be a mere ghost-town. The convincing signage and inviting Main Street gives way to little but desert beyond—the empty void of a half-theology that never delivers what it promised (except to the charlatans who front it) and simply can't contend with reality.

So what about embracing the suffering, then? The Buddha said that life *is* suffering. Maybe we just need a good dose of realism? But, to only see the suffering is to ignore the promised victory. Faith is dissolved by functional atheism that claims to contend *with* suffering by letting go of God's antidote *to* suffering—the victory of the resurrection. And, if we're honest, sometimes we are functional atheists. Letting go of promised victory makes us cowards—afraid to risk stepping out in faith because we're convinced it probably won't work. We don't ask for healing because we've seen so few. We don't share our faith because it probably won't work. Like a self-fulfilling anti-prophecy, it proves itself true, and so we keep ourselves here. Faithful living is not about gritting our teeth and getting through. And a poverty gospel is no more faithful than the prosperity gospel it disdains.

Here is the biblical way forward—the way to hold victory and suffering in bold, biblical tension.

In Victory, Remember the Suffering

Perhaps you're reading this and things are going really well. The college acceptance letter came in, you got the raise, the baby finally learned to sleep, or you finally met that special someone. You saw the conversion you've been praying for, witnessed the healing that cannot be explained, or feel the power of the Spirit's presence. We must always allow suffering to augment our joys, and the journey to adjust our victories.

"Wait," you say: "You want me to remember *suffering* on my happiest days?"

Yes, but probably not quite like you think.

When we experience bliss in this life, we Christians must stay tethered to the story in which we experience that bliss. We say, "God thank you for this beautiful day," not because we are trying to forget the cloudy days but precisely because we *remember* them. The enjoyment of the sun on our face is increased by the memory of the days when the rain hits our brow. We rejoice on our wedding day because our souls contrast that with our lonelier moments. Mothers laugh with joy at the birth of their children through the shouts of pain in childbirth. We are more grateful for our victories when we remember that suffering is also a part of life. And we are more humble in our victories when we remember that they are not all of life.

Were we to try to see victory as the "right" and "only legitimate" parts of life, working hard to erase the memory of pain, we would do something very unnatural, and contrary to the means by which God has ordained humans souls to grow. As Nassim Taleb points out in his book *Anti-Fragile*, there are certain things that are neither fragile (they break easily) nor robust (they don't break at all). Some things are anti-fragile:

"Antifragility is beyond resilience or robustness. The resilient resists shocks and stays the same; the antifragile gets better." [23]

The human soul is an anti-fragile thing, and God brings suffering into our lives not only because we've fallen off the path of righteousness (though that will certainly bring suffering) but sometimes because we're squarely in the middle of it.

So, when things are going well (and I hope they often go well for you), remember by what contrast it is that you know them to be so good. Few things are as unhealthy to our souls as constant success, riches, glory, and fame. Such things have the ability to make us forget the road that got

---

23 *Anti-Fragile: Things That Gain from Disorder* (Random House, 2012), Kindle Loc. 321.

us there, and (much worse) to forget the cross Christ bore to bring us even greater riches, which require us to shoulder our own crosses too.

In Suffering, Remember the Victory

Just as constant victory can cause us to degenerate into thankless, entitled children, constant suffering can cause degeneration in the other direction—towards self-pity, despair, pride, and worse. We might spite God and others because of our pain, or we see our pain as somehow meaning we are better or superior to those who have not borne what we have borne. While God will use pain and suffering as a tool, he promises a future where these will no longer be necessary. These thoughts are constantly with me, even in present suffering.

Practically, that means cultivating a habit of thankfulness though tears. I am thankful that things will not always be this way. I am thankful that Jesus understands suffering. I am thankful that, though he will likely win some battles, my enemy will lose the war. While the previous point of remembering suffering in our victories may seem counterintuitive, the inverse is more obvious. When we suffer in the valley of the shadow of death, we must remember that victory is just ahead—and that the enemy is a defeated one, flailing before his final loss.

This was the entire motivation of Paul's celebration of the resurrection in 1 Corinthians 15:

> "When the perishable puts on the imperishable, and the mortal puts on immortality, then shall come to pass the saying that is written: 'Death is swallowed up in victory. O death, where is your victory? O death, where is your sting?' The sting of death is sin, and the power of sin is

the law. But thanks be to God, who gives us the victory
through our Lord Jesus Christ." (v 54-56)

When our resurrection is at hand, death isn't just defeated
by victory. Death is swallowed by it—metabolized, even.
In the Christian story, the suffering of Jesus on the cross
is the righteous road of Psalm 23. Goodness and mercy
followed Jesus all the way into the tomb, and brought him
out again, raising him to dwell with his Father forever.

When your child isn't where you wish they were, when
the marriage dissolves, when disease comes, when
disappointment stalks—do not acquiesce to the nihilistic
belief that it will always be this way and that God is neither
present nor particularly good. The resurrected Jesus
resoundingly declares that God is both better than we
imagine and at work to eliminate suffering. Let the cross-
tomb tension of suffering and victory free you to produce
from this light, momentary affliction a weight of glory
beyond all compare. Easter Sunday follows Good Friday.
That's why Good Friday, with all its blood and splintery
suffering, is still, somehow, good.

Forge the Virtue of Unconquerable Faith

I still love to sing those words, "We got the victory!" And I
still believe them. Only now, I think I believe them better.

As we've seen, there is much to lose if we let go of this
doctrinal tension; and there is at least one great thing we
will gain if we do not—unconquerable faith. Such faith isn't
unconquerable because it is loud but because it is deep.
It doesn't break easily because it was forged in a hotter
furnace and cooled with better water. That is exactly what
Paul expected would happen. I quoted the apostle above,
but not his final words in that chapter. He already told us

how the mysterious merger of suffering and victory are resolved in the cross and resurrection, and then he tells us what that produces:

> *"Therefore, my beloved brothers, be steadfast, immovable, always abounding in the work of the Lord, knowing that in the Lord your labor is not in vain."*
>
> *(1 Corinthians 15 v 58)*

Steadfast, immovable, and unconquerable faith abounds in work for the Lord. We can abound, too, if we have eyes to see. Sometimes, abounding looks like victory tempered by suffering; other times it looks like suffering but persevering, with eyes on the victory. Always, we are accompanied by the presence of God the Spirit, the same companion who never left Jesus through his best and worst moments.

If you navigate this cross-tomb, suffering-victory tension as a central part of your apprenticeship to Jesus, you will become faithful in the ways he was. You will live expectantly and boldly, asking for great things and stepping out to do them. And you will live steadfastly and resolutely, walking through pain and difficulty with present stability and future hope. Then, in the furnace of suffering and the waters of victory, God will forge unconquerable faith in you.

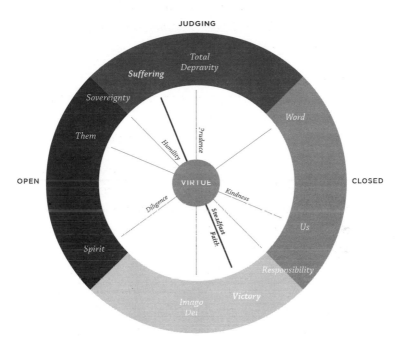

6. LOVE *AND* WRATH

"He that has no charity deserves no mercy."
English proverb

"A god of kindness would be charitable to all. Your god of wrath and punishment is but a monstrous phantasy."
Emile Zola

"**L**ove is love," proclaimed the banners.

Pride week was in full flow, and amorous language was as ubiquitous as the rainbows. This new international holiday creates understandable consternation on the part of Christians, still recovering from the whiplash induced by a rather quick cultural shift on sexual ethics. But in this particular Pride week I was particularly vexed: not by the holiday per se, but by the conversation I heard coming from some of its celebrants. Sitting in my favorite local coffee shop, I was pondering my upcoming sermon... on love, of all things. This tension—God's love and God's wrath—was rolling around my head and heart like a marble. But the marble came to a halt when I overhead the group sitting at the table near me.

"Look," my rainbow-clad, Americano-sipping neighbor said to his friends. "God is love, right?"

No one at the table answered right away, so he continued.

"I grew up in church, and it's true. God is love: the Bible says so."

"So far, so good," I thought. My neighbor had read 1 John. Or, at least, heard someone who had.

"And if God is love, then there's no way he hates us, or anything about us. A God of love would empathize. He would never judge, like some Christians think he would. Jesus said we shouldn't judge. Love doesn't judge."

His emphasis on the word "doesn't" still rings in my ears.

Their conversation carried on, but my attention didn't. I was fixated on that sentence, "Love doesn't judge." Buried in that axiom was a theological proposition: if God is love, then God is not angry. Love doesn't judge.

Conversations like this are common across many coffee shops, I'm sure. The next story, however, is less common.

"God hates fags!" the signs shouted.

Westboro Baptist Church had struck again, callously canvassing the funeral of Matthew Shepherd, a young man from Laramie, Wyoming who was beaten to death by two men, allegedly because he was gay. This group—which ironically is neither Baptist, nor a true church—had made the effort to come along in order to spew hatred.

"Burn in hell!" shouted one picketer, sign in hand.

"God hates you," announced another.

In the grief of loss, I cannot imagine the injury such false Christians caused Matthew Shepherd's family and friends. The deity they serve is angry and isn't loving much at all. And they, becoming what they worship, horrify everyone else with their hatred and view it as faithful obedience.

Two stories, two gods.

So, will the real deity please stand up?

TWO TALES, ONE TENSION

You probably read the first story with more sympathy than the second. Given the triumph of cultural progressivism, we in the West are more comfortable with an affirming deity who never condemns than an angry one who does. The second tale is more shocking to the liberal mind. Westboro Baptist is no church of the Lord Jesus, after all. The false god of hate to whom they pay homage surely has nothing to do with the God who is actually there, right?

Right...

But ask yourself which tale offended and annoyed you, and why. To which group would you extend mercy? Diagnostically, this is useful for idolatry detection. Why idolatry? Because at different times and in different ways, we all bend the knee to both of those false deities. Consider the following entirely possible parables:

- Cut off in traffic, obscenities fly out of your mouth at the motorist that preferred his speed over your right of way. Peaceful evening commute interrupted, you're now all adrenalin and outrage, the steering wheel serving as the lone witness to your verbal tirade. Taking a breath, you shake your head at your fellow motorist, in an "I can't believe that just happened," sort of way, when you feel a tinge of conviction. Good thing the guys from the Bible study didn't hear all that, eh? "Well," you reason, "God loves me. He's a God of grace, after all."

- It's election night, and you're anxiously watching the results come in. You try to play it cool, but between the talking heads on the television and the pontificating personages on social media, it's becoming difficult. At some point, it becomes clear—your side has lost. Shocked, you react to the victory laps those people are taking. Taking to social media to let the full measure of your wrath out, you soothe yourself with the knowledge that God is on *your* side, as you decry the depravity of opposition. After all, they're worthy of your hatred because God's probably not too pleased with them either.

- "Get in the car! We're going to be late!" you shout to your son, trying to hide the panic in your tone. He just made the travel team, after all, and you want him to make a good impression. Between music lessons, homework, and sports, you know he's feeling the pressure. Oh, and then there's church. "Mom, I miss my friends," he says, looking out the window.
  "Youth group is every week, honey. Your team needs you," you reassure him.
  But you wonder... Is that tinge of guilt you feel conviction, or... well, never mind. Church will still be there next week, but today there's a game. God understands. He's a God of grace, after all...

- On the first night of that business trip, you flip through the channels as you settle to bed. Unexpectedly alighting upon the kind of explicit film you've worked hard to avoid, you scoff.

"Disgusting," you say. "I can't believe people film this stuff." So, you flip past it.

And then you return.

Your eyes lustfully drink in the images on the screen, leading you down a too-familiar road, the end of which promises pleasure but produces only shame. Your now-gripped heart convicting you, you tell yourself, "God is love. He forgives. It's not that big of a deal." You tell no one, and after a while the sense of guilt fades—just like it always does.

These examples—and a hundred others—could be any of us. Twin impulses betraying twin idolatries: a pinch of incense to the false god of love followed by a bow to the false God of hate, depending on which side of things we find ourselves on—sinner, or sinned against. Grace for me but not for thee. Judgment for thee but none for me. The situations change, but the self-deceptive two-step is the same: we all struggle not to hate certain folk while simultaneously believing we deserve love and forgiveness. We do it every time we soft-pedal our own sin... every time we deride "them"... every time we indulge our flesh... every time we indict our neighbor. And when we do, *we* are sitting at that table in the coffee shop, and *we* are holding up the banners. We walk from side to side, consorting with the false god of love or hate according to which deity makes us feel better.

WHAT IS LOVE, ACTUALLY?

Avoiding the shallows of both counterfeit love and retaliative, proud anger requires us to define our terms. Love and wrath evoke such powerful emotions that we risk back-loading feelings into our view of God—a truly terrible way to proceed. To me, the word *love* conjures up my feelings for my wife and kids (and for a good pizza), while the word *wrath* brings forth the image of an abusive father stomping down the stairs in a fit of rage. The feelings these terms conjure are important, but they're no substitute for biblical definitions. So let's get a handle on these words.

Distilling a biblical definition of love is a challenge.[24] The Bible records romantic love, parental love, brotherly love, and love for God, just to name a few. In his book *The Four Loves*, C.S. Lewis famously drew the distinction between four kinds of love: *eros*, a romantic love; *philos*, friendship love; *storge*, love for things like pizza or baseball; and *agape*, a God-type love characterized by sacrifice in pursuit of another's greatest good. For the sake of this brief chapter, we'll home in on that last one and set our definition of love as God's *affectionate, unstoppable commitment to the good of his people*.

Like love, wrath is also a challenge to pin down. Anger is described in all sorts of ways in the Scriptures; most instances of it are not good because most of the anger in the Bible comes from us. Happily, God is not like us. God's wrath is connected to his holiness and justice, not unmeasured self-centeredness. Because he is totally committed to the good of his people, he is totally opposed to whatever threatens that good. So, we can define the wrath of God as *God's holy, unstoppable determination to destroy that which threatens those whom he loves*. Clear definitions in hand, let's explore this tension together and learn how to hold it as faithfully as the Scriptures do.

---

24   For more on this, see D.A. Carson, *The Difficult Doctrine of the Love of God* (Crossway, 1999).

THE UNEXPECTED ENTANGLEMENT OF LOVE AND WRATH

Have you ever noticed that the people who make you the most angry and hurt tend to be the very people about whom you most care? If, as you cross the street, a random stranger shouts, "I hate you" to you, you'd find it unpleasant, but hardly damaging. But let your spouse say those same words and a response of pain and anger will be unavoidable. Surprising as it may seem, love and wrath are not rivals but relatives. Suppose you have a teenage son and he is arrested for driving under the influence of drugs or alcohol. You'd be angry. And you should be. Only an *un*loving parent wouldn't be. Suppose your beloved long-time pastor was caught stealing church money. You'd be angry. And you should be, precisely because you loved him and trusted him. The more you love someone, the more you will feel wrath and rage for their foolish and sinful choices.

It's important that we understand—especially in light of our cultural obsession with safety, anti-bullying, trigger warnings, and the like—that wrath is not wrong. Psychologist Gary Chapman puts it like this:

> "Anger is not evil; anger is not sinful; anger is not a part of our fallen nature; anger is not Satan at work in our lives. Quite the contrary. Anger is evidence that we are made in God's image; it demonstrates that we still have some concern for justice and righteousness in spite of our fallen estate. The capacity for anger is strong evidence that we are more than mere animals. It reveals our concern for rightness, justice, and fairness. The experience of anger is evidence of our nobility, not our depravity." [25]

---

25 *Anger: Handling a Powerful Emotion in a Healthy Way* (Moody Publishers, 2007), page 23.

This isn't merely true psychologically, but theologically. D.A. Carson notes:

> *"One evangelical cliché has it that God hates the sin but loves the sinner. There is a small element of truth in these words: God has nothing but hate for the sin, but this cannot be said with respect to how God sees the sinner. Nevertheless the cliché is false on the face of it, and should be abandoned. Fourteen times in the first fifty psalms alone, the psalmists state that God hates the sinner, that his wrath is on the liar, and so forth. In the Bible the wrath of God rests on both the sin (Romans 1:18-23) and the sinner (1:24-32; 2:5; John 3:36)."* [26]

As counterintuitive as it seems, Carson is exactly right. Love and wrath are inextricably linked. Think about Adam and Eve. God lovingly nurtured our first father and mother in the womb of his tender care. Yet the very ones he loved he also cast out. Angry at their rebellion and promising the pain that would follow them (Genesis 3 v 8-24), the God of love opposed his beloved because they had chosen sin. Perhaps most strikingly, God revealed the heart of his character to Moses by announcing:

> *"The LORD, the LORD, a God merciful and gracious, slow to anger, and abounding in steadfast love and faithfulness, keeping steadfast love for thousands, forgiving iniquity and transgression and sin, but who will by no means clear the guilty, visiting the iniquity of the fathers on the children and the children's children, to the third and the fourth generation." (Exodus 34 v 6-7)*

26   "God's Love and God's Wrath," Bibliotheca Sacra 156 (1999): 388–390.

How are we to understand this? It is, as we've grown to expect by now, a tension.

As odd as it may sound to Western ears, saturated as we are in the cloyingly sweet positivity of pop psychology, safetyism, and success, God's love and wrath toward sinners are simultaneous for him. They go together—a fact we overlook at our peril. The belief that God cannot possibly love people and burn with wrath for them can only grow in the security and ease of a polite Western landscape. We imagine that God is as much of a helicopter parent as we're told we must be. By importing popular parenting advice into our inner theologies, we've convinced ourselves that God would never oppose us and love us... right?

Such simplicities don't fit with the Scriptures. The God they describe is no progressive-politics-approved deity, affirming and embracing with no anger for sin. Neither is he the hateful behavior-police—so zealously offended by our brokenness that he can't wait to torture us in hell. Such imitation deities are neither worthy of our devotion nor helpful in any real situation. The real world is far more complicated and much better. He's neither pushover nor power-mad. He is the God of charity.

MEET CHARITY

To the modern imagination, the word "charity" conjures images of money for the homeless, pocket change for the Salvation Army, or serving meals at the local soup kitchen. But, from heaven's viewpoint, it's something very much more. It's the merciful, costly grace of God, which rises from his wrath and love—a mercy for the spiritually poor like you and me.

The word rises from the Old French word *charité*—a very Christian word for mercy and compassion. And *that* word arises from the Latin *caritas*, meaning "costliness, esteem, or affection." It came to be the favored English word for—you guessed it—*agape*: that particular kind of love with which we're concerned in this chapter. And that kind of love can only come from a God who simultaneously has *a holy, unstoppable determination to destroy that which threatens those whom he loves* and *an affectionate, unstoppable commitment to the good of his people*. Only the biblical tension between love and wrath could create charity.

Let's state this clearly: God loves sinners, *and* God is opposed to them. He cares for them even while he stands against them. But how can this be? The first half of that sentence offends both our pride and our justified desire for justice, and the second our progressive sensibilities. His love for us is tangled up with his justified anger toward us, because he's a very good Father. We must hold these twin convictions intentionally if we're going to build the virtue of charity. God has a holy, unstoppable determination to destroy that which threatens those whom he loves *and* God has an affectionate, unstoppable commitment to the good of his people. How can these both be true?

Because of the cross—God's cosmic demonstration of charity.

> "In this is love, not that we have loved God but that he loved us and sent his Son to be the propitiation for our sins." (1 John 4 v 10)

The word used here for "love" is *agape*—charity.

Look at the cross. Look deeply. The intersection of its splintery beams are the precise location in time and space where infinite love and terrible wrath met. With open-wide arms, Christ welcomed the sons of Adam and daughters of Eve, all through blood-stained wood grain and wrath-bearing screams. "God shows his own love for us in this: that *while we were yet sinners* Christ died for us" (Romans 5 v 8, my emphasis). Exodus and promised land, judgment and judges, kingdom and exile, exile and return—the themes of God's love and God's wrath increase in severity and solemnity throughout the whole Old Testament and reach final expression at the cross. Here is where God's love and wrath finally meet—at the cross: God's torturous, gracious instrument of charity.

As the Son of God stared up at that splintered tree, he was filled with *affectionate, unstoppable commitment to the good of his people.* As nails split apart the same hands that formed our first father, he was experiencing his own *holy, unstoppable determination to destroy that which threatens those whom he loves.* Love and wrath met in his own body that he might resurrect and forgive you and me. He, the just justifier of the ungodly (Romans 2 v 26) didn't oppose sin in some theoretical way, but by pouring his wrath out upon his Son, who bore our sins on the tree (1 Peter 2 v 24). Sin didn't die on the cross; Christ did. Sin didn't bleed, didn't cry, didn't gasp for air under the torturous weight of terrible wrath. God's own Son did. For us. Because he loved us. His cross was his cosmic demonstration of his charity toward us.

The cross simultaneously shows us God's wrath against sin and his love for sinners—love and wrath. The God of the cross is better than the wannabe deities of love and hate. The God of the cross loved unto death, and died unto love. And those of us who worship him must learn to do the same.

LOVE AND WRATH IN REAL LIFE

The Catechism of the Catholic Church defines charity as that virtue "by which we love God above all things for his own sake, and our neighbor as ourselves for the love of God." As definitions go, that's a great one—loving God for who he's shown himself to be in Christ and extending that same love to our neighbor. But the question remains, how does holding on to this troublesome tension help us hone this particular virtue?

In our age of rage, charity is a virtue great in both rarity and demand. To a culture that kowtows to the false god of love, charity says, "I love you *even while* I oppose your view and way of life." And to a culture that too frequently runs on the fast-burning fuel of hate, it says, "I oppose you, but I still love you and want you to join me in the way of grace and life." This is the love-wrath way of charity. This is what rescues us from the rage of the false God of judgment-alone, and the impotence and injustice of the false God of everyone-and-everything-is-fine. He's not a God who changes with shifting cultural norms, and so we are freed to hold fast to truth. Neither is he a God who delights in destructions, and so we are freed from both that exhausting posture of hatred and a hateful posture of pride.

So, how do we grow the virtue of charity?

Repent of Your Rage

I don't know what others do that enrages you, but I'm sure something does. Whether you express it like I do, with shouting and bluster, or internalize it like others do, with bitterness and dismissal, you need to turn from these patterns. This starts with seeing what the role of anger is biblically. It moves to identifying the ways that you experience or express anger wrongly. It may involve good counseling and help, professionally. But we need to move past our innate god-of-hate idolatry. Love your enemy and pray for those who hurt you.

Repent of Weak Love

Love is both an emotion and a decision. You cannot conjure up the first, but you can determine the second—and the first often follows the second. Decide to love others in the way Christ loved you. Weak love is a wonderful strategy to seem nice, but it will rob you of true intimacy and the experience of God's love. Christ wept over his friends, laughed with them, and served them with all he had. And he told them when they were in the wrong. What do you need to change to love others like that? Perhaps it begins with a fresh biblical vision, some honest conversations, and a few new disciplines. Stop affirming sin or keeping silent about error for the sake of peace. Love others enough to disagree. Yes, humbly; yes, gently; but yes, firmly. Weak love is cowardly—a self-centered pride that cares more about human opinions than God's. Christ cared more about people than popularity, and so should we. Perfect love casts out fear and makes you strong. Speak the truth, whatever it costs.

Pursue Your Healing

The lies we've believed and the pain we've received will tend to produce either weak love or reactive rage—and, in most of us, both. In this chapter, I've worked to displace a few common lies, but my words can't heal your pain. Some of you reading this have been truly traumatized. Abuse, racism, abandonment, war—there are many ways we can receive soul wounds in this sin-shattered world. Repentance and forgiveness are decisions, but pursuing healing takes discipline and discipleship. Talk to your pastor or find a wise mentor (or both), and get a plan. Then pursue the healing which Christ died to give you. This takes a church family and the power of the Spirit. So, wherever you're wounded, start the journey of healing.

Practice Charity

The charity demanded by God's love and wrath cost him everything. The dissonant harmonies resolve on the cross. So, when they swell in you, you must remember the cross, and bear it too. For the victims of racism, sexism, bigotry, and hate, charity's cross will cost dearly. But faithful, biblical living will remind you that, at times, you've been a victimizer too. God's love-wrath gave rise to cross-shaped charity that has been extended to you. So you must extend it too. Sometimes we just need to step forward into it, praying that God would change our hearts as we do. So with faith in Christ and wisdom from God's word, find a way to extend charity specifically to those whom you find most challenging.

LOVE AND WRATH IN *MY* LIFE

We began this chapter with stories about others. We'll end with one about me.

My earliest memories—good as well as bad—bear stains of the substances that mastered those closest to me—alcohol, drugs, even work and success. Their addictions impacted me in ways that I didn't deserve, couldn't avoid, and eventually resented. If you've ever been close to an addict, you may be able to relate to the profound frustration and anger I felt watching my family hurt themselves, manipulate others, and break bonds of trust in the pursuit of substances that could never satisfy, and never did.

For this, I hated them.

I came to despise those I was to love and trust. There was no "hate the sin, love the sinner." I was incapable of such an idealistic response to incessant pain. And if I'm honest, I suspect all of us are. We might be able to separate sin from sinner out of a vague, conceptual love for humanity in general, but not when it comes to humans who are meant to protect us and yet hurt us. When someone you love with all your heart breaks it, simplistic platitudes prove too weak. "Love the sinner, hate the sin" sounds like something Jesus said. But he never did.

Those words weren't God's, but Gandhi's. A nice guy, I'm sure, but not a Christian. Let's think twice about embracing the ideas of Gandhi as if they were the ideas of God.[27] I'm not suggesting that we should foster and feed a deep anger toward those who sin against us. I'm suggesting that it's impossible not to. Impossible for us, and inadvisable. Anger is an appropriate response to evil and injustice. It's how God feels toward evil, and how we should as well.

Yet, even while filled with justifiable anger at my family, I still loved them. Somehow, they all held the deepest parts of my heart at the same moments when I held them in deep derision. My real, raw love for them didn't negate my

---

27 The phrase "hate the sin, love the sinner" is not found in the Bible. An early form of this idea may have come from Augustine of Hippo in a letter he wrote to a commune of nuns (Letter 211, c. 424). In this letter he encourages them to "act with love for the persons and hatred of sins." But more recently, Mahatma Gandhi wrote this in his autobiography, saying, "hate the sin and not the sinner is a precept which, though easy enough to understand, is rarely practiced, and that is why the poison of hatred spreads in the world."

gut-level opposition to them. If anything, it fueled it. The contrast only made love that much more real.

Anger is a gift from God given as the right response to evil and injustice.[28] However, it's also a powerful emotion, easily twisted into hate. I had to forgive my family, walking through a journey of healing from the trauma of my childhood which took years. Yet the antidote was not a limp, weak affection that overlooked the wrongs. "Love is strong as death" (Song of Solomon 8 v 6), and looking back I see that there were times when I did not love my family with an affectionate commitment to their good but only with a convenient politeness to preserve the peace. I've learned— and am continuing to learn—to love my family, lean in, and serve them at a higher cost to myself—without ever saying that the wrongs didn't matter.

THE HAPPY TENSION OF THE LOVE-WRATH OF GOD

This is a tension that we mustn't jettison. After all, it's the core of our gospel. The Jesus-event—his life, death, and resurrection—is incomprehensible without love and wrath. If God is not wrathful toward sinners, Jesus' death is a mere inspiring tragedy. If God is not loving toward sinners, Jesus' death is the shock-and-awe reaction of a malevolent deity. God's determined opposition to that which will destroy those whom he loves is what drove him to demonstrate, at great cost to himself, his affectionate, unstoppable commitment to the good of his people. For those of us who have embraced the love-wrath of the cross, faithfully holding that tension in our dealings with others is a non-negotiable requirement of faithfulness. Whether

---

28   See Gary Chapman, *Anger: Handling a Powerful Emotion in a Healthy Way*, page 23.

it's in the coffee shop, or seeing the placards. Whether it's at the wheel, on election night, with the kids, or flicking through the channels—we must learn to worship the real God: the God who hates sinners *and* loves sinners. That will see us live more faithfully toward him and more charitably toward others—whoever they are.

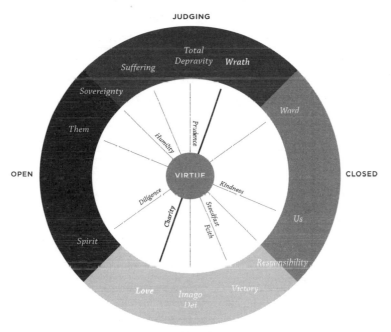

7. POLITICS *AND* KINGDOM

"The idea that religion and politics don't mix was invented by the devil to keep Christians from running their own country."
Jerry Falwell

"Church and state should be separate, not only in form, but fact—religion and politics should not be mingled."
Millard Fillmore

I was 16 when I discovered talk radio.

Enjoying my newfound freedom as a driver, I was searching for something to listen to. As podcasts had not yet been invented, the "scan" button on my car radio did its magic, and I stumbled into the world of American conservative politics. As I was catechized by its exponents on my drive to school, my identity as a Christian and my politics as a conservative became more enmeshed the more I listened. All was clear, and very firm, in my mind.

Until college, that is.

And no, I didn't meet some atheist professor who turned me into a full-bore socialist. Instead, my fragile but fervent equilibrium was disrupted when I met someone, in my church, who loved Jesus and who was—brace yourself—a Democrat.

"A disciple *and* a Democrat?!" I scoffed.

To my twenty-year-old mind, this was not possible. I had been taught by my talk-radio teachers that Democrats weren't just wrong about policy but were wrong existentially. So I set about helping her discover what I already knew—that she was wrong, Jesus voted Republican, and she needed to repent, urgently.

As we interacted, I discovered that her story was the inverse of mine. A white man with successful parents, I had gravitated toward the conservative emphasis on personal responsibility, national identity, freedom from tyranny, and economic prosperity. As a Christian, I found that much of socially conservative morality appealed to me. My argument was simple: if we could free more people from the dithering "help" of government, they'd bear up under the weight of their own existence, take responsibility, grow morally, and experience the blessings of liberty.

My friend was a black woman raised by a single mother in constant poverty, and so she had understandably gravitated toward the liberal emphasis on social responsibility. To her ears, phrases like "national identity" and "economic prosperity" were thinly veiled euphemisms for Jim Crow 2.0—a subtle and underhanded sequel to the overt racial discrimination of previous generations. While she personally embraced a "conservative" morality, she saw hypocrisy in the political captivity of the mostly-white churches who desired to use the power of government as a tool for the gospel. Her argument was simple: if we could equalize society through government intervention, groups who were left behind could take their place in a fairer society and experience their share of the blessings of liberty—blessings that had been too long kept from them by a rigged system.

I was not prepared for the reasonableness of my opponent. Many discussions ensued, some better than others. But neither of us moved, which was frustrating. Eventually, frustration boiled over in one particular discussion. Losing patience, we reached for the final weapon of the anxious politico—the *ad hominem* attack. We both started to play the man and not the ball. We both said things to each other that brought more heat than light, more pain than productive dialogue. Unable to agree, we settled for aggression.

Later we apologized, but we didn't talk politics much after that. In fact, we didn't talk much at all. I suspect we both still thought we were right. Convinced that the fate of our nation was in the balance, we found it easy to let passion get the better of us. She graduated, moved on, and, I suspect, still thinks very much like she did. Why wouldn't she? Her last memory of a white, male, Christian conservative was one who was unkind to her. As if cast for the role of political villain of progressives, I played the part beautifully. Still, I came out of it feeling right. And all it cost me was Christian unity.

FLAWED DIAGNOSIS, FEARFUL REACTIVITY

Don't take this story as the virtue-signaling confession of someone plagued with white guilt. My left-leaning interlocutor said her share of harsh words too, and I still have strong opinions on basically everything (though many have changed from those days). I regret my unkindness, of course—but that's not really my point here. I am *more* unsettled by how unthinkingly we bought into the lie that made the whole mess possible: that we are supposed to be moving toward a better future in our land, and that politics is the most important way to get us there.

That is a lie; and when this lie is embraced, even the most well-meaning Christian will over-function with anxious political activism. Why? Because his well-being is enmeshed and entangled with the well-being of the state— and specifically, with *his* vision for it. If his party wins, he wins. If it loses, he not only loses but faces an existential crisis. It's not just that he's not ok; he cannot be ok. Why? Because he's relocated his peace from the unchanging promises of God to the changing winds of politics. Believing a flawed diagnosis of the problem—namely, that the *other side* is keeping us from progress or threatening our foundations—he fizzes with fear-filled annoyance that sometimes froths up in anger, even though he's meant to be a Spirit-filled person of peace. How can a pastor pour televised hate on his political interlocutor? Because he's imbibed the lie that politics can deliver heaven or threaten hell. How does a disciple disown those who are politically different? Because she's bought the falsehood that policy brings ultimate peace and safety. And we do the same. We sing to God on Sunday and spit vitriol on Monday because deep down we believe the right president, prime minister, or parliamentarian has power to save.

Our political tribes divide up the church, and the angrier we get the louder hell laughs.

In his brilliant 2007 book *A Failure of Nerve*, Edwin Friedman prophesied our anxious age a decade before it came to be. He understood our networks of relationships as "family systems." He observed that nations, businesses, political parties, teams, and families are each kinds of family systems. And, when "[unhealthy] families get fixed on their symptoms ... rather than on the emotional processes that keep those symptoms chronic, they will recycle their problems perpetually no matter what technical changes they make, how much advice they receive from experts, or how hard they try to understand their symptoms."[29] In other words, when a family system—be it a church, office staff, or nation—has malfunctioning members, we fixate on fixing the malfunctions, dialing up the anxiety in that system of interconnected relationships, and ensuring the system is never actually fixed. In the cause of political systems this is especially clear. Presuming that we have a right to constant progress, we tear ourselves increasingly asunder, anxiously striving to rid ourselves of this or that politico, position, or political party, ironically ignorant of the real problem: our misdiagnosis of the problem.

It's a brilliant strategy really. Satan masterfully catastrophizes socio-political realities, manipulating us Christians to seek to turn stones into bread, so that we faithlessly fight over solutions to problems that aren't the real issue. We fail to do what Jesus did: to see through Satan's temptation to satiate fear with power. In the desert, emaciated after 40 days without food, Jesus' body was shutting down, crushed with hunger. What did he think at this moment? What did he fear? Since he was fully human and tempted in every way even as we are (Hebrews 4 v 15), it's not unreasonable to imagine that he was tempted to think, *I'm going to die. This isn't going to work. What was I thinking?* In Jesus' weakest moment, Satan tempted the Son with anxiety—the emotion of unbelief. *Your Father*

---

29 *A Failure of Nerve: Leadership in the Age of the Quick Fix* (Church Publishing Inc., 2017), Kindle Loc. 1149.

won't come through. Your path of holiness and self-sacrifice will never work. I rule this world, and to win around here, you play by my rules. By lying to our Lord, he sought to inject anxiety into the first Family System: the Trinity.

But the God of peace cannot be duped into mistrust within himself. Jesus resisted, and hell was silent. Angels came, and so did the kingdom of God.

ADVOCATING ON EARTH, ACHING FOR HEAVEN

Because Jesus understood the actual problem, he resisted the temptation to solve a false one. We would do well to follow his example. The problem is not now—and was not then—with right or left, progressivism or conservatism, but in the conflict between the politics of this fallen world's kingdoms and the kingdom of God.

God's people struggled to grasp this even when the long-promised Savior-King walked among them. Jesus was neither Sadducee nor Pharisee, neither a Herodian nor a Roman. His opponents' greatest frustrations with him, and a major cause of his friends' regular confusion about him, was his refusal to pick one of these sides and live as though the triumph of that side mattered. It turned out that God was concerned with more than mere politics: with restoring his people into his presence. Yet God was not—and is not—about a milquetoast, tepid middle way between political parties, or about a retreat from worldly politics altogether. He's about the actual tension—the one between heaven and earth, between present politics and his promised kingdom. As we'll see, only by holding fast to the latter can we faithfully hold the former.

Why is this a tension? Because read one Christian thinker and the Bible sounds like a this-worldly text about political engagement; read another and it is an other-worldly text advocating peaceful *dis*engagement. Read the Bible yourself and it sounds like both, at different points. Some Scriptures are *literal* laws that were to be enacted within a nation, Israel; others are prophetic reminders that God is above *all* nations. Jesus came as the Savior-King of one tribal nation: Israel. Yet his mission and message are about making a *new* Israel from among *every* tribe and nation. As with the other tensions mentioned in this book, we need to remember that this isn't an accident: the Spirit knew he was doing this to (and for) us. So let's explore how.

From the beginning, creation is a political project. To "be fruitful, multiply, fill the earth, and subdue it," (Genesis 1 v 28), Adam and Eve were to literally create the *polis*—the people, who were to be under God's loving rule. But after sin's disruption, humanity sought make good on this mandate apart from the presence and rule of God. And by Genesis 11, we find humans are building *Babel*—a city with a great tower constructed in defiance of God's command to "fill the earth." Babel was a political project, too, attempting to rewrite the story of human progress without the God of the story. God scattered its builders, saving them from the work of their own rebellious hands. Then, through the patriarchs and the exodus, God led his people towards his land. He gave to Moses the project of organizing this society into godly civil governance. In the Torah—Israel's origin story and legal code—God himself wrote the laws that would govern his people. And for brief moments, the hope of a body politic to reboot Eden looked promising.

Yet over and over again, the project failed. Israel was disciplined in exile, and things got complicated. The same God who commanded them to be so distinct from other

nations that they weren't even to mingle fabrics (see Leviticus
19 v 19 and Deuteronomy 22 v 11), much less worship their
gods, now commanded them to seek the good of other
nations—even those that took them captive (Jeremiah 29
v 5-7). God's promises through the prophets pushed beyond
Israel's borders to the very places that subjected Israel. God
would judge other nations (Jeremiah 46 and Isaiah 15 – 23,
for example), yet God would include them in the Messiah's
kingdom (Isaiah 52 v 15; 55; 56 v 1-8), refresh them through
a future temple (Ezekiel 47), and freely give his saving Spirit
to anyone who called upon his name (Joel 2 v 28-32).

In Jesus, these prophecies came to pass, the Messiah
simultaneously fulfilling God's promises to a particular
nation and his invitation all nations (Acts 2 v 14-41; Romans
9 – 11). He gave his Spirit to Israel (Acts 2) *and* to Israel's
enemies (Acts 10). The Scriptures commanded Christians to
be model citizens for maximum gospel influence (Romans
13; 1 Timothy 2 v 1-4), yet to remember that their citizenship
and security were in a world to come (Philippians 3 v 17 –
4 v 1). As we saw in chapter 4, Peter calls his readers "elect
exiles": a reminder that they should care about this world as
those who are preparing for the world to come.

What's a Christian to do with this? Wash our hands of this
world and its politics? Or increase our political advocacy,
influencing our respective nations with the values of the
kingdom to come? I want a simple answer, I truly do. But we
must beware. For, our impatience for biblical solutions and
sensible progress—even "kingdom of God" progress—makes
us susceptible to idolatrous ideologies that are crouched and
waiting to devour the politically passionate. So before we
chart out God's political platform, let's expose these ideologies
and—more importantly—their insidious common source.

BABYLON OR BUST

I vividly remember the election of President Obama in 2008. I was living in the UK at the time, but the feeling of euphoria was powerful enough to be felt even across the pond. His campaign watchwords were "hope" and "change." For many Americans, electing our first black president felt like a pivotal moment in history whereby we put to death our national sins of racism and made a promise to our children for a better tomorrow. Following his inauguration, many felt sure that we'd stepped into a new historical epoch of peace, hope, and promise. At the time I also very vividly remember feeling terribly bad for our new president and for the people who'd placed such hopes in him—not because I disliked him but because there's only one Messiah powerful enough to bring about true hope and change, and he doesn't say the Pledge of Allegiance. There was no way for any man to do what Obama had promised or what his supporters had hoped.

I also vividly remember the election of President Trump in 2016. By now we were living in Boston—the cradle of American liberty—and there, the misery was palpable. Harvard canceled classes, protests erupted, and I found myself pastoring people through things I never imagined an American election could provoke. Following his inauguration, the same electors who were previously certain we'd elected a political Messiah were equally certain we'd elected a political anti-Christ, and that the destruction of America, if not the world, was imminent. Like the last time, I remember feeling terribly bad for our new president, and for the people who had now placed such devilish fears in him. Why? Because there's only one judge who kicks off the last days, and he's not a billionaire from New York. The anxiety they felt was as exaggerated as the greatness he was promising.

Probably something about those two paragraphs offended you. (Perhaps both did, simply because of the focus on the US. To which I say, sorry—I can't speak into every political situation. But what I can do is encourage you to substitute your country's versions of Obama and Trump. Fearing and fawning over political leaders are not uniquely American phenomena.) I can hear some of you thinking, "You can't compare Obama to Trump!" Or "Obama ruined the economy." Or perhaps "Trump's rhetoric encourages racists!" But before getting your undergarments in a twist, wait. Notice what you're doing and what you're feeling. My point here is not to commend or critique these men and their politics—even though I have my own opinions—but to comment on what our collective anxiety, defensiveness, and offendability tell us about ourselves: namely, that we've believed the lies that we are supposed to be moving toward the better future of freedom—toward progress— and that politics is the most important way to get us there. Hell is just one election away, so let's get saved by getting registered and getting out the vote.

If you and I believe that about politics, there's no way we can believe the best about our brother or sister who thinks differently.

Should we invest hope in politicians? Sure, a bit. Should we fear politicians? Sure, a bit. But the all-out war that many Western democracies have turned elections into can only be explained by the prior belief that politics is the primary means by which we obtain the promise of progress. We're drunk on the promise of progress, so we stumble from politician to politician without the sobering benefit of biblical foundations to inform our beliefs. As the pastor and sociologist Mark Sayers puts it, we want progress without God's presence.[30] We expect the golden streets of the future kingdom without the King.

Now, that's excusable if you don't know the King, but it's unthinkable if you do. Yet we so often go along with this anxious, tribalistic vitriol, blissfully unaware that we're playing right into the same lie that Babel's architects believed—that we can get back to heaven on earth if we just build the way ourselves.

To modern readers, the story of Babel induces a chuckle. Who, after all, thinks you can get back to heaven with a brick-built tower? And it is laughable, to be sure. But is that any more laughable than thinking you can bring about utopia through better healthcare or education? Through better technology and prosperity? Through a better military or foreign policy?

We're no better than Babel's builders. We just have more advanced bricks.

God in effect knocked over the little Tower of Babel, but frustratingly, we keep rebuilding bigger versions of it. In the Bible, Babel grew into Babylon—a kingdom of power, violence, wealth, and false worship. And God's people, Israel, couldn't help but act like the Babylonians. Instead of using power to protect and serve, Israel's kings ended up using it to oppress and subdue. Instead of using wealth for worship, Israel ended up worshiping wealth. Instead of worshiping Yahweh and building lives upon his presence, they worshiped other gods and trashed the temple. Eventually, God concluded that if his people loved

---

30 *Reappearing Church: The Hope of Renewal in the Rise of our Post-Christian Culture* (Moody, 2019), page 91.

Babylon so much, they could move right in, and he exiled them there.

A remnant of exiles eventually returned to the land, but the feeling of their exile remained. Then King Jesus came. This king used power differently—other kings killed their enemies, but this king was killed for his enemies. He used wealth differently—other kings hoarded wealth and taxed their subjects, but this king lived in poverty to give his subjects streets of gold and indestructible treasure. Other kings demanded to be worshiped as gods, but this king emptied himself of such rights to reveal to the world that he really was—and is—God, and to deal a death blow to every other spiritual being that was pretending to be God.

By the end of the Bible Babylon has grown, metaphorically, for in Revelation it represents all kingdoms that misuse power, wealth, and worship. And Babylon is thrown down (Revelation 18), just as its first tower was. Those who loved the wealth and power of Babylon more than God's kingdom weep (Revelation 18 v 11-14), but the saints, who long for the kingdom of God, rejoice (Revelation 19 v 1-5).

Such is the destiny of all Babylons—all political systems that promise the kingdom without the King, a new creation without the Creator, and progress apart from God's presence. God is determined to knock down our towers, again and again. He loves us too much to let us live in Babylon forever. But when our favorite Babylon—be it on the right or left—gets knocked down, what does our weeping suggest? Perhaps that we're too similar to the tearful Babylonians in Revelation 18, and not similar enough to the singing saints of the next chapter.

Jesus said, "the gate is wide and the way is easy that leads to destruction" (Matthew 7 v 13)—and when it comes to politics the wide road is an eight-lane super-highway. That's because eventually every politician and every party make promises that only God can deliver.

Pause. Reread that sentence. Yes, since the days of ancient kings, human leaders have been elevated over their peers in the belief that they will make the tribe, the kingdom, the nation, or the world, better. Better is the goal. Better is our destiny. Better is our right! Right? Be they conservative or progressive, monarchist or populist, powerful or poor, our rulers have repackaged the same Babylon campaign slogan: "Give me money and power, and your loyalty and trust, and I'll make it all better." Promising freedom, they imprison us to serve their political ends. Promising peace, they conscript us to fight neighbor and family to win political wars. Promising rest, they demand of us constant work to vigilantly guard the borders of accepted speech and ideas. Promising heaven through technological, moral, economic, and medical progress, they fall short as technology brings increased division, invasion of privacy, social isolation, and cultural disintegration.

None of this means we're not called to seek the good of the city—Jeremiah wrote that to exiles living in *literal* Babylon. We can't turn our backs on politics, wash our hands, and feel virtuously pure about our disengagement, holding out for the second coming. Godly men and women are needed in politics. It does mean that, to greater or lesser degrees, every country is Babylon, and it can't coexist with the kingdom. It also means we'll never find a perfect leader, leading the populace with all strength and virtuosity. Living as both citizens of the kingdom and inhabitants of Babylon—and seeking the good of our political body without doing so idolatrously—is a tension.

WELCOME JUSTICE

Earlier I asked, "What's a Christian to do with politics?" We've seen how the Scriptures knowingly guide us to an answer by means of the tension between Israel's political journey and Jesus' ultimate kingdom authority. Knowing this, and embracing this tension, will grow in you the virtue of justice. Justice means defending the righteous and condemning the guilty, by advocating for laws reflecting a kingdom morality, and can only result from seeing heaven and earth rightly. If we never look heavenward, we won't know what is right. If we disengage politically, we'll never do what is right. But if we hold both in tension, we'll embody what is right. That is justice—rightness and righteousness before God and others. So, let's see how justice is grown in us as we hold this tension faithfully.

Kingdom Purity, Not Political Purity

Being a faithful disciple of King Jesus and a citizen in a Western democracy requires you to live out a kingdom purity *instead of* a political one. Put simply, if you're more conservative (or progressive) than you are Christian, you're not actually a Christian. If you can quote Burke and Limbaugh, Marx and Bernie, but struggle to locate the book of Malachi, you'll need to rethink your priorities. If you feel more commonality with a non-Christian who shares your politics than a Christian who disagrees with them, you have a problem. And if you hold politicians you oppose to a different standard than those you support, then let's call it what it is: unjust hypocrisy. These are all signs that you've got more political purity than biblical fidelity.

Kingdom purity means saturating yourself more and more in the stories, values, and sensibilities of the Scriptures. It means being actively discipled in a church family, where you may find (as I did) that not everyone agrees with you, politically. All this helps you develop a biblical view of the world and a kingdom identity. Justice, after all, is the property of just One. The Scriptures are his act of self-revelation, and must therefore be a primary object of our attention and devotion. If we don't read them faithfully, we'll never understand politics rightly.

Political Discernment

To discern means "to cut apart." As you and I let go of ideological purity to embrace kingdom purity, we'll grow in our ability to cut apart the promises of politicians and their parties. Here are a few questions I've learned to ask as I seek to engage with politics faithfully:

- Is a false promise of progress that only Jesus can bring about being made?

- How is this platform/politician trusting human strength and savvy in opposition to faith in God's good sovereignty?

- How am I being told to use power? For revolution, resistance, and oppression; or for service, love, and reconciliation?

- What is the "prize" I'm being offered? Is it a false freedom to do what I want, or a true freedom to love and serve God and neighbor?

Spirit-Filled Advocacy

Please don't mistake me for someone who thinks about politics cynically. Governments are important God-ordained institutions with responsibilities to protect what is good, foster peace, and execute justice (Romans 13). The people of God have a responsibility to advocate for God's wisdom and God's ways in these domains. But we must do so filled and led by the Holy Spirit. Historically, there have been good examples of this—William Wilberforce's leadership in the abolition of slavery, or Martin Luther King's nonviolent resistance in the pursuit of justice for black Americans; along with tragic examples of not doing this—American churches giving theological cover for racism and slavery. We mustn't assume that simply because we are Christians we are advocating God's ways. We must listen to the Spirit and be careful to read the Bible well, humbly listening when we might have gotten something wrong. If we think things are simple when it comes to Christian political engagement, it's likely we're off-beam. And we must test ourselves by asking, "Is my political activity marked by good spiritual fruit?" The Spirit will produce love, joy, peace, patience, kindness, goodness, faithfulness, gentleness, and self-control. If such fruit isn't present, the Spirit probably isn't either.

Prophetic Witness

Whenever the church has fallen captive to a political ideology, God has seen fit to raise up a prophetic voice to call us back to true justice. In early 19th-century England, it was Wilberforce. In 1930s Germany, it was Bonhoeffer. In 1960s America, it was MLK. There are plenty of issues of profound injustice about which God is heartbroken and angry. From human sex-slavery to incipient racism, from political genocide of peoples to the preferential genocide of abortion, we can—and we must—engage for change without exchanging our souls. For if we do not engage over these issues, we may have already lost them. The way is narrow, to be sure. But the way is necessary for the sake of the world—both the one today, and the one to come.

Prophetic truth-telling is not license for social-media trolling, speaking rudely, or forcing obedience of every nuance of Christian morality through the power of civil authority. In his book *Center Church*, Tim Keller describes how the gospel comes to affirm, confront, and console parts of every culture.[31] Consider your natural political bent—what in it would the Scriptures affirm? What would they confront? What parts should be completed and consoled by the gospel? Go on and speak prophetically, but only in a measure equal to your willingness to listen to such prophetic speech yourself.

Reconciliatory Posture

In every election, and in every political action, there are winners and losers. And our posture when we win and when we lose is most important to our witness. If we approach political engagement painting the other party as the enemy, then victory will create a feeling of superiority—our side won, and now we make the other side pay. But, as ethicist and political theologian Russell Moore suggests, "If what differentiates us [from the world] is blood poured out for our sins, then we see ourselves for what we are: hell deserving sinners in the hands of a merciful God."[32] We have been given the ministry of reconciliation (2 Corinthians 5 v 18), which

---

31 *Center Church: Doing Balanced, Gospel-Centered Ministry in Your City* (Zondervan, 2012).

32 *Onward: Engaging the Culture Without Losing the Gospel* (B&H, 2015), page 9.

means the nature of our political activity (and everything else for that matter) must have reconciliation as its aim— reconciliation both to God and to each other.

I call this a posture because sometimes reconciliation can take generations. In the case of my own country's sins of racism and slavery, I've had to learn that racial healing and reconciliation is a journey for my black and brown brothers and sisters. Whether it's winning a local election or correcting a generational injustice, the heart posture of the people of God must be reconciliation with, not cancelation of, our political "enemy."

We all need to develop the discipline of putting down the phone, stepping back from social media, and saying no to intra-Christian political rows that help no one. Taking offense is not a virtue, and fighting foolishly is not for Christians. You'll get an email, a text message, a comment, or a cross word that beckons you into the ring. And when it comes, ask yourself, "Is this the kind of fight Jesus would fight?" If you're not sure, consult the Scriptures, call your pastor, and cry out to God. Correcting the fool on Facebook probably won't change his mind as much as it will twist your soul. Reconciled reconcilers shouldn't show up to sub-Christian scuffles.

Future Hope
Your candidates are going to lose some elections. Embrace it, accept it, and for God's sake (literally) get over it. While the world may lose their collective marbles when an election goes "wrong," may it never be so for the church of Jesus Christ. When you feel the nagging draw of anxiety on election night, remember your King is on the throne already. While the outcome may change the moment, it

changes neither the mission nor eternity. The world is desperate for a people who are secure enough in grace that they can flourish under Caesar, whoever he or she may be. Trust Jesus, receive peace, and refuse the anxiety that betrays an innate political idolatry. And if you find yourself in a state of panic, slow down enough to ask why. Confess your fear to the Lord and to the family of God, and call out for the courage to move forward. Jesus at times was afraid (Luke 22 v 41-44), and at other indignant (Luke 19 v 45-46), but he was never apoplectic. His hope was in the future victory promised by his Father. Ours is too.

AN AMAZING OPPORTUNITY

In my city, depression and anxiety are on the rise. Political radicalism and division are rising too. While I hate the increase in these pathologies, I'm beginning to see that they present the church with an opportunity. The promises of our political programs—that more wealth, more power, and more technology will lead to more freedom and happiness—are failing. Babylon's glossy brochure isn't producing. Like compost on the forest floor of our culture, the detritus of discontent is decomposing into an opportunity for gospel seeds to grow. For those who have eyes to see, it's an amazing time to be a Christian in the West. With love in our hearts, truth in our mouths, and the Spirit in our midst, we can see a great harvest of righteousness, peace, and justice. Truth and grace always lead to change, and when the soil is fertile, the change could be monumental.

What might our progeny write about this moment? That we won elections, or that we were part of an awakening of new Christians? Politics won't save our civilization. But the people of Jesus may just transform it into something that looks a bit more like the kingdom to come.

Young Adam Mabry was anxious and insecure—threatened by difference and thorough in his dismissal of those with whom he disagreed. Young Adam would have fitted in well in the second decade of the third millennium. Driven by the anxious diagnosis of a non-problem to fight battles for a non-solution, some of us fall victim to folly. But we don't have to. Embracing the biblical tension between present politics and the future kingdom, we can develop the virtue of justice not only in ourselves but in our cultures. The only question is: will we be open to the searching of the Spirit and the scalpel of the Scriptures?

If we were, how different our nations might be.

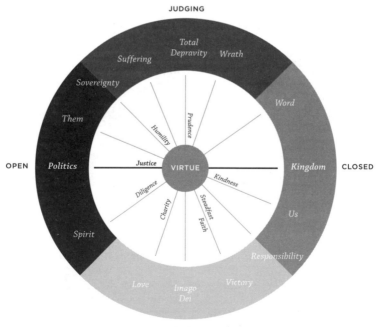

8. STRONG *AND* WEAK

"Power! Absolute Power!"
Emperor Sheev Palpatine, Stars Wars Episode III

"Great men are almost always bad men."
John Dalberg-Acton, 1887

I almost didn't write this chapter. Not because I don't think it important but because I want to take sides here. Why? I have a "strong" personality.

Whenever I do a personality test—whether it's Myers-Briggs, DISC, StrengthsFinder, or enneagram—they all say the same thing: hardwired, in charge, extroverted, and commanding. I'm a self-starter—entrepreneurial, a leader, a do-er. I'm highly driven, and I drive others quite hard. This personality has helped me a ton. But it's gotten me into trouble as a Christian, too. Many word-wounds inflicted by me and upon me have led me through much repentance and therapy. Turns out that holiness and assholey-ness aren't quite the same thing.

But then there's Jesus. I can't help but imagine Christ sitting across from me sometimes (though probably not often enough). When I do, I see a man far more powerful than me dying willingly for his enemies. And I can't help but imagine Jesus looking over at me—a person far weaker than he—and see me enjoying power a bit too much. And that—that mental picture—really challenges me.

It messes with the way I wield this personality of mine.

It turns upside down how I think about the church in the world, and the kind of church that I want to lead and be a part of.

And it's starts to foster a virtue in me that I never really wanted: namely meekness—a meekness that, though still in seed form, surprises no one more than it surprises me.

POWER STRUGGLE

The Bible says a lot about the power that is innate in human beings. God created the world by his own power and created us humans to rule it (Genesis 1 v 26-28). Sin and its effect in the garden was about much more than fruit and fig leaves—it was about a power struggle in the unseen realm (Ezekiel 28 v 17; Isaiah 14 v 9, 11–12, 15).[33] One of the spiritual beings God created sought the power and status that belonged only to God, and in seeking it he was cast out of God's presence, taking those he duped with him.

The rest of the Bible chronicles how humanity, after listening to Satan promise us God-like power, use their God-given power in all the wrong ways. By the end of the first eleven chapters of Genesis, humans had marshaled their ingenuity to construct Babel (Genesis 11)—a towering

---

33 For more on this see Michael S. Heiser, *The Unseen Realm: Recovering the Supernatural Worldview of the Bible* (Lexham Press, 2015), Kindle Loc. 91.

monument to humanity's determination to be in charge, to take the decisions, to drive forward their own agenda.

Though God thwarted the rebels of Babel, the power struggle marches on today. Babylons are built with the bricks of human power: Egypt, Assyria, Babylon, Rome, and every empire since—each built by human power apart from God's presence, and each trampling the feeble, enslaving the poor, and conquering the weak. Empires came and went, but the *modus operandi* remained the same: wield power to get more power.

Strangely, into this power struggle, the most powerful Person was born as the most powerless kind of person: an infant son of a poor, teenage Jewish girl. And this was the climax of God's plan for his world.

I wonder what those rebellious spiritual beings thought when Christ was born. Were they confused? Worried? Triumphant? Whatever they thought, I'm sure they didn't see this plan coming. This Jesus, protected from the initial threat on his life by fleeing to Egypt, was moved back to Israel when matters seemed to cool, and lived rather anonymously. Likely taking up the trade of his adoptive father before carrying out the work of his heavenly Father, he must have seemed like a failure to such beings. Furniture-maker, wood-crafter, home-builder—sure. Anointed King, conquering Savior, serpent-crusher—not so much. Perhaps they were tempted to think God a bit of a fool. Much ado about nothing...

Then came the day of his baptism.

On that day, the most powerful Person partook of the one rite that made the least sense—baptism. Joining his relative John the Baptist at the waterside, he watched sinners sacramentally wash in the waters of repentance—

it was the ultimate admission of spiritual powerlessness. Those who came (and come) to baptism's water came (and come) as sinners: the spiritually dead, morally powerless, and ethically impotent. That's why John was so shocked that Jesus would come and ask to be baptized. With a symmetry that was no accident, the same Savior who would end his mission in weakness and death began his ministry with its symbolic version.

As the Son emerged from the water, things changed. The Creator spoke from heaven: "This is my Son" (Matthew 3 v 17). And at that moment, the rebellious ones in the spiritual realm realized that things were not as they seemed. The Spirit took him to the desert, where the devil was waiting for him. All the lies of the enemy had one temptation in common—power. *Jesus, use your power to satisfy your hunger. Jesus, use your power to manipulate your Father. Jesus, give me your power to get even more.*

What a strange situation that must have been. Jesus— the incarnate Son—could have, with the mere movement of his will, caused the devil to simply fall out of existence. With the word of his mouth he could have called down angelic armies. So, with all that power at his disposal, what did he do? He stayed hungry, thirsty, and tired, quoting the writings of men weaker than he. This, too, was a symbolic symmetry. The devil's first defeat would be through Christ's weakness and faithfulness. And the devil's final and far more devastating defeat would come the exact same way.

ALL POWER DIES

The events surrounding the death of Jesus seem even more unlikely. (It's only our familiarity with them that blunts the shock.) Matthew's account acknowledges as much: "Do you think that I cannot appeal to my Father," Jesus points out to his enemies, "and he will at once send me more than twelve legions of angels?" (26 v 53). To the Roman governor, Pilate, the most powerful man in the province, he effectively says, *Oh I'm a ruler, all right. But not like you are... My kingdom isn't a this-worldly one* (John 18 v 33 – 19 v 11). Jesus could have said, *Ok, that's enough,* spoken a word, and summoned thousands of warriors clad in light who would fill the skies, laying waste God's enemies. If I'm honest, I would have done that.

Jesus didn't (you knew that). The real story isn't a Hollywood script, and the real hero isn't an action star. In a plot twist no one expected, the all-powerful one experienced things that he has no business experiencing: weakness, pain, torture, and death. In short, powerlessness. Jesus breathed his last, and hell must have roared with laughter.

Day one.

Day two.

Then—praise God—day three.

Death's exhalation gave way to the breath of new life in God's new world. Hell's laughter must have twisted into a confused furore. The moment of greatest weakness had become the weapon by which the Lord of lords had defeated the so-called powers of this world.

And that is how the early church turned the world upside down: not through strength but weakness. Hell threw everything at the infant church, as it had at the infant Savior. Mockery. Persecution. Exile. Court summons. Kingly inquisitions. Imprisonment. Disappointment. Betrayal. Death. Suffering of all kinds. But they knew, as Paul reminded the Ephesian flock, that they had a different kind of strength: that they were called to "be strong in the Lord and in the strength of *his* might. Put on the whole armor of God ... For we do *not* wrestle against flesh and blood, but against the rulers, against the authorities, against the cosmic powers over this present darkness, against the *spiritual forces* of evil in the heavenly places" (Ephesians 6 v 10–13, emphasis mine).

Fight? Yes. Be strong? Certainly. But not by throwing around the bricks of Babel.

ON THORNS AND TOUGHNESS

Paul understood power. He was a Roman citizen—a big deal. He had power, access, and privileges that most residents of the Roman world lacked. Not only that, but he was also a Pharisee—he had standing and heft in the Jewish religious system. Strength and influence—that was the currency. As a younger man, Paul was surely looking for a Messiah who would better the brute force of Rome. Small wonder, then, that when an upstart sect of fellow Jews started to insist that this weak, Galilean rabbi was God's promised deliverer, Paul was incensed. Hold a few coats while their owners stone the infidels? Sure. Seek out these insurgents and bring them to justice? Absolutely. He was granted the power to pursue, persecute, and prosecute the followers of this false prophet. And that's what he set out to do.

Then the suffering, weak Messiah met him—in awesome power—on the road to Damascus (Acts 9). No longer the bleeding peasant on the cross, the resurrected Messiah spoke from his throne, and Paul was changed. His privilege would be exchanged for a perilous promise: you will suffer for my name (Acts 9 v 16). From one perspective,

Paul became one of the most powerful and influential humans in history. His movement, his letters, and his work still shape the world today. But from another angle, this powerful person became sad and weak. He was imprisoned, abandoned, betrayed, tortured, and finally martyred. His life of fruit and faith was also marked by a thorn, which he described in his written correspondence with the Corinthian congregation:

> *"So to keep me from becoming conceited because of the surpassing greatness of the revelations, a thorn was given me in the flesh, a messenger of Satan to harass me, to keep me from becoming conceited. Three times I pleaded with the Lord about this, that it should leave me. But he said to me, 'My grace is sufficient for you, for my power is made perfect in weakness.' Therefore I will boast all the more gladly of my weaknesses, so that the power of Christ may rest upon me. For the sake of Christ, then, I am content with weaknesses, insults, hardships, persecutions, and calamities. For when I am weak, then I am strong."* (2 Corinthians 12 v 7–10)

Paul, the great apostle, embraced weakness, walking in the way of his Lord. And then he was strong. But how, exactly, did this weak-therefore-strong tension work for Paul? And more to the point, what did it produce in him? And how on earth did weakness make God look powerful? Before we can answer those questions, we need to look at what's at stake if we get this tension wrong.

WUSSES AND WINNERS

My grandpa once told me, "Adam, there are wusses and winners. Don't be a wuss."

Historically, this wuss-or-winner tension has been divisive, even in (perhaps especially in) the church.

As committed pacifists, the early church were very open about their refusal to participate in the power of Rome. They refused military service, celebrated martyrdom, and saw themselves as faithfully trusting in the coming Savior, who would mete out the punishments in his own time.[34] But all that began to change after Constantine embraced Christianity (AD 312). Suddenly, the persecuted minority became the privileged majority, and some Christians sought to propagate the faith by means of the threat of the state. Sadly, once the church hierarchy got a taste for power, it tended to compromise to keep it. The church was on the path to justifying such extreme measures as multiple crusades, crushing dissent, burning books, and withdrawing the Scriptures from common people so that power could only reside in the priesthood. The Reformation period was no better. Instead of wielding power against pagans as it had done, the church turned on itself. Long wars between Catholics and Protestants are scars on the testimony of the church that still damage our witness in certain parts of the world. Live by the sword, die by the sword, it seems...

But must we live with such a choice? Must we be wusses or winners? No. Was Jesus a "winner?" Not really. As N.T. Wright often points out, if the messianic horse you were backing ended up dead on a cross, that would be an indication that you'd backed a loser, not a winner.[35] But

---

34 See Kirk R. MacGregor, "Nonviolence in the Ancient Church and Christian Obedience," Themelios 33, no. 1 (2008): 16.

35 "Jesus, Israel and the Cross," originally published in SBL 1985 Seminar Papers, ed. K.H. Richards (Scholars Press, 1985), pages 75–95.

Jesus wasn't a "loser," either. He's not dead but alive, his resurrection having achieved the greatest victory ever won. Was Paul a "loser?" Sort of. He walked away from an up-and-coming career in the Roman-Jewish power class. But by becoming such a "loser," he won victory after victory, soul after soul, in city after city. Winners or wusses? With all due respect to my grandpa, this isn't a choice we have to make. "For when I am weak, then I am strong" (2 Corinthians 12 v 10). Or as Jesus put it, "Many who are first will be last, and the last first" (Matthew 19 v 30). After all, his kingdom is not of this world, and neither should his followers' use of power be:

> "You know that the rulers of the Gentiles lord it over them, and their great ones exercise authority over them. It shall not be so among you. But whoever would be great among you must be your servant, and whoever would be first among you must be your slave, even as the Son of Man came not to be served but to serve, and to give his life as a ransom for many." (Matthew 20 v 25–28)

The Christian's relationship to power and weakness isn't straightforward, and it isn't binary. If it were a dating relationship, we'd say "It's complicated." Since it's a theological concept, we say it's a tension—a dynamic relationship between power and weakness where power is not what the world counts as power, nor weakness quite what the world counts as weak. The history of the church shows us that misunderstanding this tension has a high price: namely, the damage of our gospel witness. Equally, the promise of Scripture shows that getting it right comes with a great reward: namely, the virtue of meekness.

MEEK AIN'T WEAK

If I'm honest, I struggle with the Beatitudes. I know I'm supposed to love them, because Jesus said them. But if you don't struggle with them, I think that's just because you've not read them. We all want the promised blessings (inheritance of the kingdom, the earth, comfort, mercy, and so on), but we don't care much for the roadmap (spiritual poverty, mourning, hunger, and so on). For me, this was especially true of Matthew 5 v 5: "Blessed are the meek, for they shall inherit the earth."

Meek? No thanks. Isn't that just King James English for "wuss"?

Perhaps the problem is that in English "meek" sounds a lot like "weak" (a problem not present in Greek). Or perhaps it's because Jesus' pale, mild, windswept hair and white-dress-wearing image etched in the stained-glass memory of the Western imagination just doesn't inspire many little boys to say, "I want to be like *that* guy." But—and this is crucial to see—"meek" ain't "weak."

Jesus elevated this word to a status that deserves our attention. Meekness does not mean weakness in the sense of powerlessness or passivity, but the gentleness of strength truly possessed. It isn't posturing to look strong, but rather the presence of one who is strong—both in character and in power—and yet doesn't insist on their own rights, humbly embraces life as it comes, and insists that God's power is sufficient to carry them through. True meekness is seen in those who could assert power but choose not to. The strong who qualify for this blessing are the strong who decline to dominate.[36] Meekness isn't the refusal to own a sword, but

---

36   See Leon Morris, *The Gospel According to Matthew* in The Pillar New Testament Commentary series (Eerdmans, 1992), page 98.

the ability to keep your hand on the hilt and the blade in its sheath, especially when the world wants you to fight. So to be meek is to be strong *and* weak.

And what is the reward for this meekness? They shall inherit the earth! It's worth pausing to really think about this. There is irony here. Our first parents lost the world by trusting the tyrant serpent. Our forebears sought fame and domination in Babel's bricks, yet were scattered in confusion. Satan promised to give Jesus the world if he'd only misuse his power, and ended up defeated and chained. Here's the irony: those who seek strength and power will lose it, while those who embrace weakness by trusting God will possess more authority and power than we've ever imagined.

The tension between power and weakness isn't some flaccid middle way. It's the conviction that God has all power and shares some of it with us, and that we wield that power not by powering up but by embracing weakness as it comes.

What might that look like in real life? In your church, it means neither insisting on politeness at virtually all costs—on servile attitudes when a "good fight" needs to be waged—nor on fighting a good fight badly. Every church member—be they pastor or parking-lot attendant—needs to be ready to have hard conversations about divorce, sexuality, gender, politics, and a whole range of other issues. Unlike mere weakness, the meek will have the hard conversations and stand their ground. Unlike mere power, the meek won't try to force or bully others to agree, winning the argument but losing the person.

In relationships, meekness means letting go of mealy-mouthed servitude *and* manipulative domineering. Some

Christians find it easy to embrace ungodly weakness, allowing others to walk all over them because they think that's what Jesus would want. Watch Jesus clearing the temple or confronting a legion of evil spirits: that's not how he behaved. Other Christians say, "Yes! Jesus spoke truth to power," and rush off to the internet to vent their rage at some politician, policy, doctrine, or church leader, never bothering to learn *how* Jesus spoke truth. Treating their spouse, kids, or employees like animals they are training instead of people worth knowing, they wield personality as a weapon.

Power tries to control a world it can't keep.

Ungodly weakness is controlled by a world with no lasting power.

But meekness is God's power in the world, and the path to humbly enjoying power in the world to come.

A WORD TO THE WEAK

I've spent most of this chapter calling us away from the wrong exercise of power. This is mainly because I have struggled most in this area. And it's not just me. The church in the West has racked up a high body count of saints who have been hurt by strong men. But at the same time, worldly weakness is as much of a problem as unrighteous strength. Worldly weakness hides, takes the easy route, blames others, and sips slowly upon the poison of self-pity. To be clear, there are victims who have been abused by the strong, and I certainly don't mean to make light of that fact. Being a victim is a terrible tragedy, and surviving that takes great bravery. But *building an identity* upon victimhood is to give in to self-pity. And to live in self-pity, for whatever reason, is not liberating nor empowering; it is cowardice.

Jesus was meek, and therefore was prepared to be weak, but he was no coward. He flipped over tables, made a whip and lashed his fellow Jews (John 2 v 13-16), rebuked a cadre of knuckle-headed, blue-collar dudes who we generally know as the disciples (Matthew 8 v 26; 19 v 13-15), and seemed to have no problem calling the most powerful people in the region wrong-headed, white-washed-gravestone sons of Satan (Matthew 23 v 27-28; John 8 v 42-45). If Jesus were alive today, some would accuse him of toxic masculinity, unjust rage, and political tactlessness. But that's what courageous, non-anxious, meek people will always be called by the cowards. But others called him soft, accusing him of giving people too much grace and not being prepared to lead (Luke 7 v 36-50; Matthew 9 v 10-13). That's what meek men will be called by the power-hungry. You can't be a meek coward any more than you can be a round triangle. Cowardice is sin, and it requires our repentance. Let this tension bring you from fear into the full-throated confession that you are weak and must be made strong, that you might inherit the earth that Christ was crushed to bequeath you.

BABYLON MUST FALL

Like I said, I have a powerful personality. But my personality is not an excuse for the wrong use of strength nor the sinful abuse of the weak. And neither is yours. If we're going to repair the damage done to our collective Christian witness though the years, including right now in our generation, we have to start to see that the surprising interaction of weakness and strength should make us neither domineering nor doormats. It should forge in us a meekness that is at once secure and strong, weak and winsome, peaceful yet determined. We must part ways with the Babylonian impulse to build towers with our strength at the expense of the weak. Doing so will mean at least these three things:

Babylon's Strategy Can't Save

If the late Middle Ages taught us that you can't convert people at the point of the sword, the late 20th century might offer the lesson that you can't proselytize with the power of politics. In every generation, there is some kind of aberrant idea that teaches that we must take power, and we Christians seem to fall for it, hook, line, and sinker.

In families, whole books are written around Babylonian strategies. For some, that looks like being a pushy parent or a manipulative spouse. Motivated out of fear and pain, we seek to build little Babels of perfect kids, the nicest household, or the happiest marriage, even if we have to cajole and control and even crush others along the way. For others, it's experienced as the spouse who controls the other through violence, be it emotional, sexual, or physical. In helicopter parents and hurtful husbands, the impulse is the same—use power to keep control, and keep control to build a high-walled kingdom of safety, security, or significance.

In churches, Babylon is alive and well. For some, that looks like pastors building their platforms on the backs of the people that Jesus gave them to pastor. Forsaking selfless service for celebrity status, these people might be social-media famous, but they might also be deeply nefarious. For other churches, it's not the pastor who is Babylonian but the people, seen in a congregational cabal of control expressed through deacons, elders, committees, and Byzantine bylaws.

For the world's nations, Babylon is the template. The biggest empire, the best economy... These can be built and used in service of Jesus, but more often than not they're just bigger Babel-bricks. As we saw in the previous chapter, the strategy of some Christians is to dominate the political scene to propagate the faith. For others, it is to abandon politics altogether and leave the world to burn. One group misrepresents Jesus as a political ruler while the other misrepresents him as an absentee father.

We cannot wield the weapons of Babylon and win victories for the Lord.

We cannot use Babylon's bricks to build the kingdom of God.

In the end, Babylon must fall (Revelation 14). If we construct our families, our churches, or our nations with its strategies, we will fall too.

Babylon's Categories Can't Help

Words matter. And the first strategy of God's enemy is always to finesse words until they mean something that God never meant. What comes to mind when you hear "power," or "weakness," may be degrees off what God means for them to mean. At present in the West, weakness is to be avoided at all costs. Yet at the same time, "power" is evil and must be wrenched from the hands of those who have it and redistributed to those who don't, under the assumption that concentration of power in one (probably patriarchal) group is evil. Supposedly, this is because the previous understanding of these two words by the so-called patriarchal system—which the present Woke-Western world is trying vociferously to overturn—is wrong. Our whole political moment is obsessed with prying worldly strength away from those who have it. It's a zero-sum game, and when God's people play it, we all lose. That is because we're playing a game with Babylonian categories.

The gospel is the story of the all-powerful One, who exerted his omnipotence through what the world calls weakness. He did this to undermine the very system of this world, down to its core—to show everyone in heaven, on earth, and under the earth that the whole game of this world is rigged and wrong.

Babylon's categories pit the worldly weak (the poor, sad, depressed, lonely, disenfranchised, and so on) against the worldly strong (the rich, powerful, handsome, beautiful, famous, and so on). We're all just trying to beat them or join them. To truly be the meek people of God requires that we reacquaint ourselves with the biblical story—and not just the parts we like. Only then will we start to think, feel, and act according to God-given visions of strength and weakness. And as we do, our growing meekness may just start to make a difference.

The implications of holding this tension are limitless (if a little scary). What would it truly look like for Christians to parent with meekness, to pastor with meekness, or to engage in politics (or even just discussions) with meekness? The insurgent king of this worldly Babylon will do everything he can to stop meekness. After all, it was the weapon that caused his greatest defeat. Using fear and fury, he will do his best to keep us at our worst—to keep you at your worst. But when you feel the anxious impulse to manipulate, control, or cajole—or to step back, back out, and duck out—just look to Jesus. Remember that this King—the true King—is meek. He—the most powerful—became weak unto death. In so doing, he defeated the ruler of the air, and he inherited the world—and he promises to give it to the meek. Every time you choose not to fight with Babylon's swords, nor to build with Babylon's bricks, you make the enemy a little weaker and the kingdom a little bigger. Our meek King has given us his Spirit to empower this in us, and bit by bit, his church is dispossessing the enemy from his territory.

If I were the devil, I guess I'd be afraid.

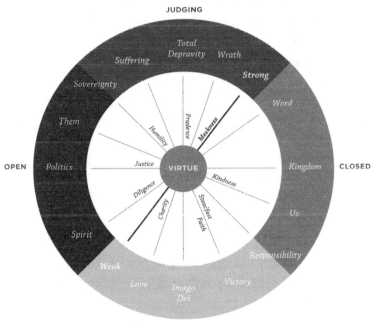

9. I
AND
WE

"*My happiness is not the means to any end. It is the end. It
is its own goal. It is its own purpose*"
Ayn Rand

"*The needs of the many outweigh the needs of the one.*"
Commander Spock

This might be the most important chapter in this book.
I saved it for last because only by passing through the
previous chapters can we be properly prepared for this one.
That's because this tension is the most confounding one of
them all: the tension between I and We.

In fact, tension hardly seems like the right word. Today,
it seems rather more like open war. Our cultural moment
is one in which a great struggle has emerged—the struggle
of *I* against *We*. And while the war between *I* and *We* has
caused countless casualties, it's usually hidden, lying
beneath smaller battlefronts. From parenting to politics,
from who we are to who we sleep with, and from societal
norms to self-help bestsellers, skirmishes rage along the

ideological landscape. And while this chapter can't solve all (or any) of those particular issues, it might just give you the key to solving them all yourself. Why?

Because when it comes to I and we, the God we serve is both.

God is *I*.

And God is *We*.

It turns out that in this sense it is God himself who is the greatest tension of all.

THE I-WE GOD

Lots of things make Christians unique. Our buildings, our music, our art, or the vision for a global, generational, every-tribe-and-tongue-and-people worshiping loudly as the second coming draws closer are all unique to us. But the most unique—and most unexpected—thing about us Christians isn't actually about us at all. It's about God. God is a God who is both radically and royally an *I*, and at the same time is a living, relational community of *We*. This is the doctrine of the Trinity, and it is the most confounding yet inspiring idea in all the Scriptures themselves.

For the Christian, the Trinity is basic stuff—or at least it should be. But I still have the words of a really smart, godly guy from a small group I led at Harvard Law School ringing in my ears: "I know I believe in the Trinity—I just don't get why it matters." Those words shook me then, and they shake me now. Why? Because nothing and no one should be more formational to you and me than who God is. And if we're being formed after a god who's not actually God, we'll be all misshapen—something which seems, sadly, to be the case quite often.

God is a Trinity. That means there is one God. Not two,

not three. One. But this one God is not like you and me. We are one thing, with one center of personhood. In fact, those two realities are so fused for us that we never consider ourselves apart from thinking about our personhood. I just talk about "me." But God is not like that. God is a Trinity. That means there are three Persons—three centers of personality—eternally existent in perfect unity. And each Person of the Trinity is God. While remaining fully aware that we cannot reach the bottom of the depths of this Trinity, let's take a brief tour of some of the foundational Scriptures upon which this awe-inducing reality is based. You may know them already, but don't let that make you skate over them complacently.

The Trinity Creates

The Father, Son, and Spirit were present, though veiled, in the first verses of the Bible. "In the beginning, God created the heavens and the earth. The earth was without form and void, and darkness was over the face of the deep. And the Spirit of God was hovering over the face of the waters. And God said..." (Genesis 1 v 1-3a). In the New Testament, John picks up on this theme and explains that God's Word is actually a person: that "God said" is a hint of another Person at work, alongside the Father and the Spirit:

> *"In the beginning was the Word, and the Word was with God, and the Word was God. He was in the beginning with God. All things were made through him, and without him was not any thing made that was made ... and the Word became flesh and dwelt among us, and we have seen his glory, glory as of the only Son from the Father, full of grace and truth ... grace and truth came through Jesus Christ." (John 1 v 1-3, 14, 17)*

The Trinity Saves

At his baptism, Jesus was given a trinitarian commission: "And when he came up out of the water, immediately he saw the heavens being torn open and the Spirit descending on him like a dove. And a voice came from heaven, 'You are my beloved Son; with you I am well pleased'" (Mark 1 v 10-11). Then, at his transfiguration, the Son stood in the presence of his Father, and was sent in the power of the Spirit to do miracles (Matthew 17 v 2-8). And, having died and risen again through the power of the Spirit to open the way back to the Father, the Son commissioned his disciples to go and "make disciples of all nations, baptizing them in the name of the Father and of the Son and of the Holy Spirit, teaching them to observe all that I have commanded you. And behold, I am with you always, to the end of the age" (Matthew 28 v 19-20). We are literally born again into the name of the Trinity.

The Trinity Shapes

For us, oneness means sameness. For God, it means unity. That's why Jesus prayed that Christian unity would be like his unity within the Trinity. He prayed that we "may all be one, just as you, Father, are in me, and I in you, that they also may be in us, so that the world may believe that you have sent me ... that they may be one even as we are one," (John 17 v 21-23).

God's trinitarian nature is what makes sense of the phrase "God is love" (1 John 4 v 8, 16). The theologian Michael Reeves points out that,

> "At bottom this God is different, for at bottom, he is not
> Creator, Ruler or even 'God' in some abstract sense:
> he is the Father, loving and giving life to his Son in the

fellowship of the Spirit. A God who is in himself love,
who before all things could 'never be anything but love.'
Having such a God happily changes everything." [37]

Cover to cover, the Bible is a self-disclosure of the Trinity—
of the great *I* and *We*. God is overflowing with love for others
precisely because he is both a unity and a community of love.
From eternity, the Father has been delighting in the Son, the
Spirit pulsating with affection for the Father, and the Son
loving the Father and the Spirit. It is precisely *this* I-and-We
God who makes us, saves us, and shapes us; it is precisely *this*
God who began history and who will bring history to its goal.
One day, the Son will be given a kingdom from his Father,
anointed by the Spirit for triune ministry as leader and Lord
of his people. The I-We God loves you and me.

But how does that help us, exactly?

Happily, since that guy raised it that morning at Harvard,
I've given it more thought.

THE I-WE WAR

In Eden, there was no competition between society and
individuality. Rather, there was harmony. Tension? Sure—
but tension like the two forces on a piano string, stretching
it into tune, to play in perfect harmony with the rest of
the strings of God's very good creation. This was the state
of *shalom*—that feature of God's nature which he gifted to
humanity, whereby each individual piece of creation was
wonderfully interplayed upon every other piece. The whole
cosmos was like a beautiful tapestry before the glorious
Trinity after whom it was formed.

---

37 *Delighting in the Trinity: An Introduction to the Christian Faith* (IVP
USA, 2012), page 38. Published in the UK as *The Good God: Enjoying
Father, Son and Spirit* (Paternoster, 2012).

But this state of affairs did not last long. Before the serpent spoke to our first mother, he was a malcontent among another order of beings—spiritual beings. Created with the same trinitarian love, these beings were granted a kind of divinity: a place in God's counsel and unseen purposes. But this being—whatever kind of spiritual being he was—fired the first shot in the I-We war. The devil, having chosen himself over the heavenly family and his own desires over those of the Trinity, aimed to tear apart the I and the we of humanity. When this mysterious being whispered to Eve, "Did God actually say, 'You may not eat of any tree...'" (Genesis 3 v 1), he said it in a way that is hidden to most of us non-Hebrew readers. To us, it seems he's quoting a command that God gave to Eve herself. So we imagine God saying, in effect, *Now, Eve, you be sure you don't touch that tree over there.* But that's not quite what Genesis 3 v 1 is saying, for here, the word "you," is not singular but plural. We might imagine it like this: *Eve,* whispered the serpent, *Did God actually keep that tree from all of you humans? All of you? Wow. He must really be holding out on you.* That's much more like the text of Genesis, and sheds a rather different light on the choice she was about to make. And Eve answers that God said that she must indeed not eat, lest humanity die (v 3).

But "when the woman saw that the tree was good for food, and that it was a delight to the eyes, and that the tree was to be desired to make one wise, she took of its fruit and ate" (Genesis 3 v 6). Suddenly, the language is all singular... all individualistic... all about her. We should read it thus: When the woman saw that the tree was good food *for her*, and that it was a delight to *her* eyes, and that the tree was to be desired to make *her* wise, she took of its fruit and ate. The Bible never mistakes its pronouns. It's telling us something important here. Eve didn't simply choose to eat the fruit because she was curious or hungry for power. *She* saw that the tree was good, not bad. *She* thought it delightful, not dangerous. *She* concluded that it was worth having. So, she chose herself over us all—over humanity. You over y'all. And so the I-We war was launched, and it rages still today—the individuals versus the collective.

INDIVIDUALISM, CALMLY CONSIDERED

No other civilization is more constructed upon the individual than that of the West. It's been a long journey from the argument of the ancient Greek Protagoras that "Man is the measure of all things." From Descartes' declaration "I think, therefore I am," to Ayn Rand's Objectivism, to Sinatra's *My Way*, the West in general and America in particular has been built upon the sovereignty of the individual. And the West isn't only constructed on philosophy. There's an awful lot of theology in our cultural basement too. God's first image-bearing creature was a human, not a group of them. Two humans formed the first family. Many families formed a society. Thus, many theologians have rightly reasoned that the individual is the basic unit of society. And that's true.

Not only that, but individuals are the basic unit of God's new society—his kingdom. Jesus—a man—came to save every individual who confesses Jesus as Lord (Romans 10 v 9). No one can repent and believe for another, and salvation is not given to groups. These biblical convictions formed the moral framework of the framers of the American experiment, with their belief that all humans were created equal and individually endowed by

God with certain rights that cannot be taken from them by a society. For those in the West, individualism is not a mere philosophy; it is a cultural birthright, and its merits are considered so obvious that they don't need to be described, much less debated.

However, individualism is not without its excess. While all humans are equal in theory, it seems, in the words of the pigs from George Orwell's *Animal Farm*, that "some are more equal than others." Sinful humans that we are, the strong have eaten the weak. The man has struck his wife, the rich have abused the poor, the boss has exploited the worker. These and a hundred other sinful excesses have given rise to a reactionary—and understandably angry—underclass. While a few have climbed their way into a worldly Elysium, they have done so upon the backs of the broken and bummed out. And when some individuals roll over others, the "others" get together, as we shall soon see.

In the church, we're not much better. We've so syncretized with our individualist culture that we "shop around for the right church" that ticks all our preferential boxes, we enjoy "worship experiences" instead of making disciples, and we live as the consumers of religious goods and services instead of the carriers of our individual crosses. We evaluate a sermon by what we got out of it; we follow celebrity preachers, especially those who contort Christ's message to center upon us. Social justice? That's for socialists. Let's talk about felt needs and my destiny, not social responsibility.

Such narcissism is soul-deep for most of us. We're more interested in self-care, social media stats, work-out routines, and our career path than the planet, her people, the poor, or the mission of God for the peoples of the world. Honestly, which would you rather (and which were you brought up to prioritize): a successful career, a good reputation, and a healthy and long life, or justice for all, in a cleaner, more gospelled world?

Individualism has important insights. But mere individualism simply can't shoulder the weight of human existence. If you care more about yourself than others, however many church clothes you dress it up in, you're guilty of the worst sin of all—pride.

But more convictingly, how can the people who worship the Trinity insist on a preference for mere individuality? Something here is amiss and it's the collectivists who have called it out.

A COLLECTION OF THOUGHTS ON COLLECTIVISM

Collectivism is the most ancient game in town. Tribal life in the ancient world was not about individual striving but the community thriving. No one was finding their real self by looking inside and following their heart. If a rogue individual put the tribe at risk, the tribe was within its rights to discipline the rogue (or worse). It was the Bible, with its doctrine that every human—no matter what they can or cannot contribute and no matter how they may have strayed beyond tribal norms—has inalienable image-bearing dignity, which was the new kid on the block.

The excesses of individualism have brought about a resurgence of the We-warriors. Whether you call it the herd mentality or your group identity, today there are whole movements purpose-built to curb the excesses of individuality and recapture a romantic vision of tribal prosperity. The globally Eastern and Southern cultures have always trended toward communal life; but I can only speak with experience when it comes to the impact of collectivism on the West. When he published his *Communist Manifesto* in 1848, I doubt that Karl Marx envisaged its impact: whole nations changed, a few dozen revolutions, innumerable class wars of different kinds, and a nuclear-armed Cold War. A century or so later, his critiques of Western individualism are still reverberating, and the We-warriors still march. Wrapped in the garb of Postmodernism, these We-warriors promise that as soon as power is wrenched from the individual and more fairly distributed throughout society, we will all finally be the good society we should have been in the first place. Today's We-warriors are usually less likely to talk about workers' rights than social justice, but the root concern is the same—justice for society and fairness for the masses, even if that comes at an expense for you or me.

And the Bible gives some support to those who march under the banner of "We." "Am I my brother's keeper?" Cain cynically asked God (Genesis 4 v 9). Jesus' answer to such a question seems to be *Of course you are!* In the story of the good Samaritan (Luke 10 v 25-37), he encourages us to care for the poor, telling us to "Go and do likewise." God's laws mandate care for the community and compassion for the poor, of course. Gleaning laws were something like ancient Israel's compulsory welfare program (Leviticus 19 v 9-18), and the whole society was oriented around the principle: "You shall love your neighbor as yourself," (Leviticus 9 v 18). God was so committed, in fact, to the community of his people that from time to time he made sure that individuals who threatened to corrupt the collective were rooted out (witness the story of Achan in Joshua 7, for example). God loved the collective enough to root out the rogues. So wasn't Spock right? Don't the needs of the many outweigh the needs of the few?

"Yes!" shout the We-warriors of our age. They fight the Me-warriors over all kinds of groups: national groups, racial groups, gender groups—the list is long. Dusting off the old ideas of Marx, some insist that collectivization of whole chunks of society will lead to human flourishing. But has it? They seem blithely unaware that the ideology with which they flirt led to the deaths of hundreds of millions in the last century. "Never mind," they insist. "This time, we'll socialize the right way." Love for humanity insists we must try, right?

And try they do, insisting that we need more social justice, more systemic change, or more global action, and that the other group (the men, the rich, the powerful, the Christians, or whoever) needs to suffer a little to make it happen. It's all done out of a love for humanity—just not that part of humanity.

Here's the thing about loving humanity: it's easy. It's human beings—the individuals—that are the problem. Humanity doesn't troll you on social media, call you a liar, break up with you, make more money than you, abuse you, or provoke your jealousy. Humans, on the other hand, do—and are very good at it. Loving humans cannot be done collectively. It must be done individually, one human at a time.

Today, the We-warriors still insist that we matter more than I. But Christians who worship and serve the Trinity never embrace such a reductionistic ideology. God is not merely a society; God is individuality. He is a Father, a Son, and a Spirit. Their individuality does not matter less than their unity. After all, Jesus said, "I and the Father are one" (John 10 v 30), not "I *am* the Father." His personhood is not enmeshed within, subservient to, or superior to the

Father's. They are different, yet they are one. Unity—but, not uniformity. I as well as we.

THE I-WE WAR IN REAL LIFE

"Ok," we might say, "I get it. But I don't see how this affects me."

I think we do. We just don't know we do.

Let me give you a few easy examples:

- When I insist that my freedom to do x (sleep with whomever I want, call myself what I want, own guns, be left alone, do drugs, live as I wish, etc.) is more important than the group's needs, I am fighting on the I side of the I-We war.

- When any democracy talks about taxation ("the rich should pay more" or "We need a flat tax" or "Tax cuts are good"), we are in fact talking about the I-We war. Do we let individuals keep *their* money or is wealth a *social* good that needs passing around?

- Any conversation about liberal/progressive vs. conservative politics is really, fundamentally, a conversation about the I-We war.

- When one side insists, "You all must change because this person must express themselves!" they are simultaneously fighting on both sides. The I side: "This person must express themselves" and the We side: "Society must shift." Ironically, (and with tremendous hypocrisy) some demand that we all must change for the sake of some individuals' oddities that have been cobbled together into a makeshift group identity. This version of the I-We war is all the rage at the moment.

Then let's take it closer to home:

- When a husband looks at porn, hiding from his wife and children, he's preferring himself—a small skirmish in the I-We war.

- When a congregation abuses the pastor's family, insisting that his wife or children live up to their standards, they're a "We" fighting an "I" in a rather unholy war.

- When a child refuses to honor their parents and goes astray because, well, they know best and no one understands them, there has been yet another casualty in the I-We war.

- When we say, "I've just got to be me," or "I'm merely living my truth," we're making a religious confession out of a view of ultimate reality— one that simultaneously expresses extreme individuality and yet demands all of the society shift around us.

So, in many ways the I-We tension is the greatest one of all. And, just like the others, it can't be solved by finding some mythical "balance," nor can it be managed by switching from side to side as our tastes change. Attempts like these always end in either selfish individualism or abusive collectivism— neither of which looks at all like heaven. The only way our individuality and society can be truly held in stability is by holding fast to the Trinity. And the Trinity, as it turns out, is precisely the prescription for war-torn humanity.

A TRINITY FOR HUMANITY

God made us in his image. So if we image-bearers don't understand ourselves in light of the I-We God after whom we're fashioned, we won't—can't—live well. And, since the I-We God is the greatest living happy tension between individuality and community, we must take our cues for living by holding this tension ourselves. The Trinity is not merely an esoteric fact; it is the foundation of all social life. When we prioritize ourselves, we're collapsing God into mere individuality. When we insist on the community's needs and ignore the least, the last, or the one who is out of cultural fashion, we reduce God's Trinity to mere uniform society. But when we hold fast to the Trinity, we completely and totally value everyone's individuality and the glorious goodness of human society. And holding this tension, as with every other tension in this book, will grant to us a virtue—the greatest virtue of all.

Love.

Love is forged in the pressure of holding fast to your individuality while willingly, and happily, laying it down for other people—even for humanity. We know this is true because that is precisely what love has done. God is love (1 John 4 v 8), and when God the Son was wrapped in human flesh, love laid down self for the sake of the world. No one forced this of him; indeed, no one could. He laid down his life willingly (John 10 v 17) for the sake of fallen humanity—the most tragic yet curiously willing casualty in the I-We battle. The perfect individual, dying for the most imperfect society. Can there be a more devastating asymmetry? And can you imagine the love that motivated it?

God is love, and he ends the war that the serpent began, not by picking a side in the I-We war but by letting the sides combine to tear him apart. The Son knew who he was—and knows who he is. He knows the Father. He loves the Spirit. But in timeless eternity, the Trinity knew the moment of sacrifice would come to pass. And the Son willingly—not begrudgingly, nor by force—purposed within the collective mind of the Trinity to become for us "the lamb slain before the foundation of the world" (Revelation 13 v 8). Collectively and individually the Trinity lovingly purposed from eternity past to save a world society composed of selfish, fearful individuals. That is love of a magnitude which will not be measured in an eternity of trying to comprehend it. And it's a love that exists precisely because God is I and God is We.

With this view of God in mind, Paul penned these immortal words to the Corinthians.

> "Love is patient and kind; love does not envy or boast;
> it is not arrogant or rude. It does not insist on its own
> way; it is not irritable or resentful; it does not rejoice at
> wrongdoing, but rejoices with the truth. Love bears all
> things, believes all things, hopes all things, endures all
> things. Love never ends." (1 Corinthians 13 v 4-8)

Theirs was a church ravaged by sinful individuality—loveless use of spiritual gifts, drunkenness during communion meals, and even some guy who'd started sleeping with his stepmom while the church community supported it and congratulated themselves for their tolerance. But look how Paul responded. He didn't excoriate them for each transgressions. Instead, he placed their transgression in the context of the I-We war and showed them their lack of love. To put it more positively, he showed them the love of God and pointed out how living like him would change them, as individual Christians and as a collective, as a church.

Holding this tension produces this kind of love in us too. Let's see how.

Patience and Kindness, Not Selfishness or Sameness
Holding the tension produces patience and kindness. When we're confronted with a troublesome person or group, our response can't be to selfishly ignore them, nor to force conformity from them. God is one and God is three, so we must be ok working with individual persons and groups of people, traveling with them on their journey of holiness, and trying our best to keep them in the "we" of God's people.

Joyful and Truthful, Not Irritable or Resentful
In the world, persons irritate us and whole groups of people merit our resentment. That guy in your small group can grate on your nerves, just like that whiny child in your home might. Whole groups of people may trigger anger or defensiveness in you—the rich and powerful, or the environmentally-exercised, perhaps? But trinitarian I-We tension forges joy and truth, enabling us to love the difficult person because we've been adopted into God's family, and to be honest when certain groups are treating others unfairly (and when they have a point). Can you imagine how different certain conversations would be if the people of God let go of self-concerned annoyance to embrace trinitarian-infused joy? What might society be like if the church wasn't resentful toward "the liberals," and instead was lovingly honest with them, seeking to win them, not beat them in an argument?

Hopeful and Enduring, Not Cynical and Abandoning
We are called to be the hopeful ones in this world, enduring light and momentary afflictions with our eyes on the weighty glory that they're producing. But too often we're cynical—which is a sad form of self-protection. The cynic who never exposes their heart is never disappointed; they're never joyful, either. The cynic is ever ready to abandon the person, or the people, who are no longer pleasing. Yet the I-We God is simultaneously deadly serious about the darkness of our situation and willing to enter into that darkness to bring us, individually, into his trinitarian society. Embrace him and we find that we are marked not by weary cynicism but by defiant hope—a hope that loves the cynic as well as those we think misguided—with our eyes firmly fixed on the possibility of a society renewed and the certainty of an eternity perfected.

These are weighty concepts. But weight is just another translation for the word "glory." And if we truly do want to see God's glory manifesting in our lives, our homes, our jobs, our churches, and, yes, our world, then we'd better get accustomed to weighty things. The I-We God is no mere single individual, nor is he a personless society. He is, gloriously, the great I-We. Difficult as it is, we must embrace this Trinity. And as we do, love will overflow from him into our lives—a love that will irresistibly change society.

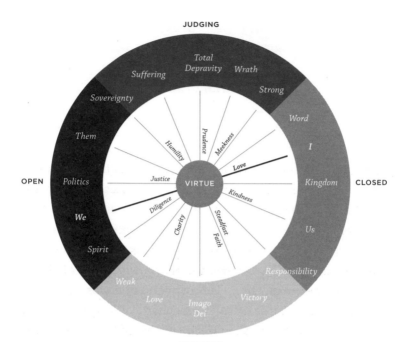

EPILOGUE

I began this book with an amusing though tragic story about two people in my church who were angry with me for not taking their side in one of my sermons. What happened next?

Well, eventually, these two people did come back to the church. In time, I arranged a meeting with each of them, and then between them. The conversation was prayerful, honest, and humble. It was also hard at times. But I'm happy to report that they both concluded that their side-taking was sub-biblical. After a few more conversations, they even became unlikely friends, and to this day—though they still have different perspectives—they're modeling to us all how partiality can give way to Christian unity.

Actually, that's not what happened at all.

The actual story has a rather sad, and much more common, ending. They both left our church. To the best of my knowledge, they're no longer in any church at all. And that breaks my heart.

I don't place the blame on them alone. I am just as susceptible to my own tribalist tendencies as the next person. I'm sure my own anxieties, proclivities, and sub-Christian preferences have leaked out in my preaching and pastoring from time to time. But that merely substantiates the thesis of this entire book: tribalistic anxiety is lodged deep in our hearts, and it tears us apart. It's a big problem for societies, but it's an intolerable state for the church. A bloody cross and an empty tomb stand as monuments to God's seriousness about uniting all things in heaven and earth in Christ (Ephesians 1 v 10). And what God brings together, no one should tear asunder.

WHAT GOD HAS JOINED TOGETHER...

Whenever I perform a wedding, I say, "What God has joined together let no one tear apart" (Mark 10 v 9). When Jesus spoke about this, he was talking about marriage, but I think these words should just as seriously (or perhaps more seriously) be applied to the church. Not *my* church or *your* church or this denomination or that institution: the Church—with a capital "C." The global, invisible, international Church. Jesus wasn't thinking of any particular tribe when he prayed for unity. He was praying for "those who will believe in me through [the apostles'] word" when he said:

> "[I ask] that they may all be one, just as you, Father, are in me, and I in you, that they also may be in us, so that the world may believe that you have sent me."
>
> (John 17 v 20-21)

Jesus' dream is that Christian unity would look like the unity within the Trinity. What's more, he tells us what is at stake—the fruitfulness of our witness. Our unity is directly connected to the world's trust in the gospel message itself.

Part of me scoffs at this prayer: "This is impossible, Jesus" or "Well, that will only be realized if those other types realize they're wrong and come over to my side." But another part of me grieves, appalled that more often than not we prefer to feel justified in the eyes of our tribe than to be loving in the eyes of our King.

CALMLY PROCEED

Recall again the graphic we've used as a guide throughout this book. Where did you start? I'm a Reformed Bible scholar who practices and believes in the continuation of all the Spirit's gifts. So, I'm starting on the right, in the closed side, right between the judgers and the intuiters. What does that mean? I need to listen hard, especially to those different than me.

What about you? Do you trend toward being more emotional? Pentecostal? Liberal? Fundamental? An easy way to tell is to ask yourself who you think shouldn't be on that list in the previous sentence. It's always easier for us to see the lopsidedness of others—and Jesus used some pretty strong language when he told a parable about that (Matthew 7 v 1-5). This is what we must resist: the judging of others before we adjudicate ourselves.

Instead, we must calmly proceed. The word calm (quite accidentally) turns out to be a useful acronym for Clarity, Argumentation, Listening, and Mystery—those tools that will enable us to stop taking sides, embrace tensions, and be free from constant fear, proud tribalism, and sprawling anxiety. If you've got liberal tendencies, remember to submit to what the Bible states clearly. If you're a feeler, challenge yourself to argue and articulate the best points of those who disagree with you. If you tend toward fundamentalist positions, listen a bit more openly, remembering that love believes the best and hopes all things (1 Corinthians 13). And if you're troubled by all of this because you like things black and white, I'm grateful that you made it this far in the book. But don't forget that the Scriptures teach us mysteries. Revel in them before you try to solve them.

HELLO, TENSION. GOODBYE, ANXIETY.

Ours is a world filled with division and anxiety. Some say it's worse than it's ever been. The good news is that though the world, and sometimes the church, keeps demanding that you take a side, you don't have to. At least, not on most things.

You needn't decide if God is sovereign or we are responsible... if politics matters or if we should just hunker down for the coming of the King... if inclusion is more important than exclusion... or if individuals matter more than societies. For these and the other issues we've discussed, side-taking is the first step on the anxious road toward division, pride, and faithlessness. Today—right now—you have a chance to turn onto a different street: a street labeled "tension" that—quite surprisingly—is a straight shot to a place of rest and peace.

The decision is quite simple, actually. Will you take the side of Scripture, which demands that you let go of sub-scriptural side-taking? Will you stand firm where the text demands it, *and* hold tensions where the text directs it, forging virtue and peace?

How can tension bring peace? Because tensions are part of what the Scriptures teach. Your responsibility—should you choose to turn onto this street—is to let go of a tendency to correct the other side, and to focus on the only matter for which Jesus will hold you to account: yourself. He will not judge me for how another pastor preached, another father fathered, or another husband loved his wife. For these things, he will judge only me. Knowing that—

truly believing it—frees me to read and wrestle with what the Scriptures say, even (and especially) when they demand that I embody a "both-and" tension to an aspect of the Christian life, rather than choose an "either-or" tribe.

Imagine for a moment what your life would be like if you did this. What virtues would you forge if you gave up tribalism? What sins would you shed if you stopped taking sides? What would your church be like if others did this with you? What would your neighborhood, town, or city be like if most of its churches loved the mission and the brethren more than the proud feeling of self-satisfaction over a point well-scored and a doctrinal scuffle won?

This journey isn't easy. Tensions never are. Tribalism is always easier and certainly more popular. You may need to put this book down and go make some amends. You might need to navigate a difficult conversation or reach out to a new group of friends. You'll definitely need to pray, asking God to shape your character through his word, by the work of his Spirit, among his people.

What if the people of God were marked by truth and grace instead of tribalism and anxiety? Don't demand that it starts with *them*—"If they'd just get it right." Start with yourself. So, as you finish this book, you have got to decide.

Not decide what side you'll be on.

But decide if you're finally ready to stop taking sides.

ACKNOWLEDGMENTS

Many people deserve my thanks for the book you've just read. First, I want to thank my loving wife, Hope. She creates a beautiful, loving, and lovely home which is the context for my life, ministry, and writing. Nothing I do could be done without her partnership. My church, Aletheia Church, Boston, allows me to test so many of my ideas upon them, and then makes room for me to reflect upon and write about them. So, to each of them—the elders, pastors, staff, leaders, and members—I am deeply grateful. Finally, I'm unendingly grateful for my spiritual family—the men and women of Every Nation Churches and Ministries. We hold onto the mission by embracing these biblical tensions, and we're all the better for it.

thegoodbook
COMPANY

BIBLICAL | RELEVANT | ACCESSIBLE

At The Good Book Company, we are dedicated to helping Christians and local churches grow. We believe that God's growth process always starts with hearing clearly what he has said to us through his timeless word—the Bible.

Ever since we opened our doors in 1991, we have been striving to produce Bible-based resources that bring glory to God. We have grown to become an international provider of user-friendly resources to the Christian community, with believers of all backgrounds and denominations using our books, Bible studies, devotionals, evangelistic resources, and DVD-based courses.

We want to equip ordinary Christians to live for Christ day by day, and churches to grow in their knowledge of God, their love for one another, and the effectiveness of their outreach.

Call us for a discussion of your needs or visit one of our local websites for more information on the resources and services we provide.

Your friends at The Good Book Company

thegoodbook.com | thegoodbook.co.uk
thegoodbook.com.au | thegoodbook.co.nz
thegoodbook.co.in